ISBN-13: 9798398561470

Cover design by: Art Painter
Library of Congress Control Number: 2018675309
Printed in the United States of America

CONTENTS

CHAPTER 1:

Personal Finance

Welcome to Money Mastery 101:
A Comprehensive Guide to Personal Finance This chapter lays the groundwork for mastering finance. Personal finance is a vast and ever-evolving field, and it's important to start with a solid understanding of the basics.

1.1 Importance of personal finances

Personal finance is the management of money and financial decisions at the individual or household level. It covers many aspects such as budgeting, savings, investments, debt management and retirement planning. Understanding and effectively managing your personal finances is critical to achieving financial stability, achieving your goals, and building wealth.

1.2 Set financial goals

One of the first steps in managing your personal finances is setting clear financial goals. Whether your goal is to pay off debt, buy a home, save for retirement, or start a business, setting specific and measurable goals gives you a roadmap for your financial journey. Consider different types of financial goals and strategies for setting achievable goals.

1.3 Cultivate a positive attitude towards money

Your mindset plays an important role in your financial success.

Developing a positive attitude towards money will help you make better financial decisions and gain control over your financial future. We discuss the importance of mindset, explore common beliefs and attitudes about money, and offer strategies for developing a positive attitude towards money.

By the end of this chapter, you will have a solid understanding of the importance of personal finances, the importance of setting financial goals, and the role of a positive attitude in your financial journey. Remember that personal finance is a journey of a lifetime, and the principles and strategies you learn here will lay a solid foundation for your future financial success. Take control of your money and get ready to embark on your journey to becoming a money master.

Importance Of Personal Finance

In today's fast-paced and complex world, personal finances play an important role in our lives. Whether we realize it or not, our financial well-being influences many aspects of our daily lives, from meeting our basic needs to pursuing our dreams and long-term goals. Understanding and managing personal finances is key to achieving financial stability, independence, and ultimately financial freedom.

Building a strong foundation
Personal finances are like the foundation of a building. Without a solid foundation, the structure will be weak and unstable. Similarly, our financial life can quickly become chaotic and stressful if we do not have a good understanding of our personal finances. By learning about personal finance, you'll lay the foundation for financial success and build a stable platform for growth.

Manage finances
Many people are living their paychecks, shouldering debt or struggling to make ends meet. This is often due to lack of financial

literacy and money management skills. By delving deeper into the world of personal finance, you will gain control over your financial situation. Learn how to effectively budget, reduce debt, and make smart financial decisions that align with your goals and values.

Make informed decisions
Personal finance is much more than just managing your money. It's also about making informed decisions. From choosing the right bank account and credit card to understanding investment options and planning for retirement, personal finance provides the knowledge to assess financial opportunities and risks. Optimize and utilize your financial resources by making informed decisions.

Plan for the future
One of the main benefits of mastering personal finance is the ability to plan for the future. Whether you're saving for a down payment on a home, financing your children's education, or preparing for retirement, personal finance provides a framework for setting and achieving long-term financial goals. Implementing an effective financial strategy can help you build wealth and build a secure future for you and your loved ones.

Achieve financial freedom
Financial freedom is the state of not having financial control over your choices and lifestyle. It means having the flexibility and resources to pursue your passions, spend time with the people you love, and enjoy life without the constant stress of money. Personal finances are the path to financial freedom. Armed with the knowledge and skills you need, you can create a solid financial plan, build your wealth, and have the freedom to live your life the way you want.

Diploma

The importance of personal finances cannot be overemphasized. It is the foundation of financial success, enabling individuals to manage their finances, make informed decisions, plan for the future, and ultimately achieve financial freedom. By embarking on a journey to mastering your money management, you are investing in yourself and creating a brighter financial future. So let's dive into the world of personal finance and discover the keys to mastering money.

Settting Financial Goals

When it comes to personal finances, setting clear and achievable financial goals is paramount to long-term success. Without a specific goal in mind, it's hard to make informed decisions, track progress, and stay motivated in your financial endeavors. This chapter discusses the importance of setting financial goals and provides practical guidance on how to set meaningful, aligned goals.

A financial goal can serve as a guide on your way to a financially prosperous life. It provides clarity and guidance so you can prioritize your efforts and make conscious choices about how you spend your money. Goal setting helps you turn your dreams into tangible goals that you can pursue and achieve. Whether you're trying to pay off debt, save for a home down payment, or retire early, you're on your way to success with clear financial goals.

Type of financial target
Financial goals can include a wide range of goals, each serving a specific purpose within the overall financial plan. Here are some common types of financial goals.

A.   *Short-term goals:*
The duration of these goals is typically one year or less. Examples include setting up an emergency fund, paying off credit card debt, and saving for the holidays.

B.   *Medium-term goals:*
These goals span his one- to five-year time horizon. This often includes saving for a home down payment, buying a car, and financing a college education.

C.   *Long-term goals:*
These goals span his five years and revolve around significant life events such as retirement, starting a business, and leaving a financial legacy for his family.

D.   *Lifestyle goals:*
These goals focus on improving quality of life and may include efforts such as traveling the world, pursuing a passion project, or achieving a certain level of financial independence.

Smart goal setting
Adhering to the SMART goal-setting framework is critical to effectively achieving your financial goals.

Specific:
Clearly define what you want to achieve. A vague goal like "Save money" is less effective than a more specific goal like "Save $10,000 on your home down payment."

E.   Measurable:
Set criteria for tracking progress. Enter a specific number. For example: B. Amount of money you want to save or percentage of debt you want to pay off.

F.   Reachable:
Set realistic and achievable goals based on your current financial situation. Consider income, expenses and schedule when determining feasibility.

D-related:
Make sure your goals align with your values â€‹â€‹and long-term goals. They should reflect what really matters to you and contribute to your overall financial well-being.

E. Expired:
Set a specific time frame to reach your goal. Deadlines create a sense of urgency and help you stay focused and motivated.

Break down your goals into actionable steps
Once you set your financial goals, break them down into small actionable steps. This approach keeps goals manageable and allows for consistent progress. For example, if his goal is to save $10,000 on his down payment for a home over two years, he can divide it into $417 per month. These small milestones give you a sense of accomplishment and keep you motivated.

Check and adjust your goals
Financial targets are not clearly set. It's important to review and adjust it regularly to reflect changing living circumstances and financial priorities. Regularly assess progress, celebrate achievements, and change goals if necessary. This flexibility ensures that your financial goals remain relevant and realistic as you navigate through life's different stages.

<u>Diploma</u>

<u>Setting financial goals is the cornerstone of personal finance. This allows you to take control of your financial future and make</u>

conscious decisions to achieve your dreams. Breaking down your goals into actionable steps by following the SMART Goal Setting Framework will get you on the road to success. Remember to review and adjust your goals regularly to stay consistent with your evolving goals. So let's set and track financial goals and begin an exciting journey to pave the way to a prosperous future.

Develop A Positive Attitude Towards Money

In the world of personal finance, understanding numbers and strategies is important, but developing a positive attitude towards money is just as important. Your thoughts shape your beliefs, attitudes, and actions when it comes to managing money. Developing a healthy and powerful mindset will prepare you for financial success and lay a solid foundation for mastering money. This chapter examines the importance of developing a positive attitude toward money and offers practical techniques for changing your relationship with money.

Feel the power of thought
Your mindset is a powerful force that influences your thoughts, feelings, and actions. It can propel you toward financial abundance, or it can drag you down into cycles of scarcity and marginalization. Developing a positive attitude towards money is very important as it shapes our financial decisions, habits and overall relationship with wealth. Changing your mindset from scarcity to abundance opens doors to new possibilities and creates a way of thinking about growth and prosperity.

Recognize limiting beliefs
Limiting beliefs are deep-seated thought patterns that prevent financial progress. Often they result from childhood experiences, social conditioning, or negative beliefs inherited from family and friends. Common limiting beliefs about money include "money is evil", "I will never get rich", and "I'm not good at spending money".

Recognizing and challenging these beliefs is an important step in developing a positive mindset. Limiting beliefs such as "I can build wealth," "I see money as a tool to achieve my dreams," or "I can manage my finances wisely." Replace it with the empowering belief of

Developing an abundance mindset

The abundance mindset is the belief that there is enough wealth and opportunity for everyone. It is a mindset that embraces the idea that one's financial success comes not at the expense of others, but rather through cooperation and prosperity. Cultivating an attitude of abundance requires shifting the focus from lack and lack to abundance and gratitude. Be grateful for the financial resources you have, focus on growth and learning opportunities, and surround yourself with positive influences that support your financial goals. adopt a growth mindset

A growth mentality is the belief that one's skills and intelligence can be developed through dedication and hard work. When it comes to personal finances, having a growth mindset allows you to view financial setbacks as learning experiences and opportunities for improvement. Embrace the idea that you can continuously learn and improve your financial skills. We view challenges as stepping stones to financial mastery and approach them with resilience and determination.

Build financial confidence

Developing financial confidence is critical to managing your finances and making informed decisions. It is a belief in one's ability to manage money effectively and achieve financial goals. Build your financial confidence by learning about personal finance, seeking advice from experts and mentors, and taking small steps towards financial empowerment. As you gain knowledge and experience, you will gain confidence and be able to navigate financial situations successfully.

Diploma

Developing a positive attitude towards money is a fundamental pillar of personal financial management. Recognizing the power of thought, challenging limiting beliefs, cultivating an abundance mindset, adopting a growth mindset, and cultivating financial confidence will set you up for financial success. Remember that developing a positive mindset is a continuous practice that requires confidence, dedication, and the willingness to challenge your beliefs. Embark on this transformational journey and develop the mindset to control your money and live a financially prosperous life.

CHAPTER 2:

Budgeting overview:

Building a strong financial base

In this chapter, we will look at the key concepts of budgeting and how it lays the foundation for a sound financial foundation. Budgeting is a powerful tool that helps you effectively understand and manage your income, expenses, and cash flow. Mastering the art of budgeting will give you the skills you need to make informed financial decisions and pave the way to financial stability and success.

Part 1:
Understand your income, expenses and cash flow

A clear understanding of your income, expenses, and cash flow is critical to creating an effective budget. Explore different sources of income such as employment, investments, and side hustle, and discuss strategies to maximize your earning potential. Understanding your own spending is equally important as it helps you identify areas where you can adjust and save money. We also explore the concept of cash flow and how it impacts your overall financial health.

Section 2:
Create a personal budget

This section will guide you through the process of creating a personal budget tailored to your specific financial situation and goals. Learn about the importance of goal setting and how it can help you prioritize your spending and savings. Learn how to categorize your spending, allocate funds for different aspects of your life, and set aside money for savings and investments. It also introduces different budgeting methods, such as the 50/30/20 rule and zero-based budgeting approaches, to help you find the method that fits your needs.

Section 3:
Track and manage expenses effectively

After you create your budget, it's important to track your spending to make sure you're staying within your planned spending limits. Learn practical techniques and tools for tracking expenses, including spreadsheets, budgeting apps, and expense tracking software. Learn how to categorize spending, analyze spending patterns, and identify areas where spending can be reduced or optimized. Effective expense management is key to staying on budget and meeting your financial goals. Section 4: Practical Tips for Saving Money

Saving money is an essential part of budgeting and building financial security. This section provides practical tips and strategies for saving money in many aspects of your life. From reducing discretionary spending and negotiating bills, to living a frugal lifestyle, and finding discounts and perks, discover practical techniques to get more out of your money. We also discuss the importance of having an emergency fund and saving for future goals such as vacation, education, and retirement.

Diploma

Congratulations on taking your first steps in mastering finance through budgeting. By understanding your income, expenses, and cash flow, creating a personal budget, effectively tracking and managing your expenses, and practicing practical savings tips, you'll be on track to build a strong financial foundation.

Understand Your Income, Expenses And Cash Flow

Introduction:

This chapter details the basic concepts of budgeting, an important tool for managing finances effectively. Budgeting gives you a clear picture of your income, expenses and cash flow. Understanding these key factors will help you make informed decisions about how to spend your money and build a strong financial foundation. Let's take a closer look at each aspect to take control of your financial life.

Understanding your income:

Income is the money you get from a variety of sources, such as work, investments, or other income-generating means. This forms the basis of financial resources and serves as a starting point for budgeting. Consider both regular income when analyzing your income. B. Salaries and Other Sources of Income.

To get a comprehensive overview of your income, first identify all your income sources and their respective amounts. This includes fixed or variable income received monthly or annually. It is important to distinguish between gross income (gross income) and net income (the amount you take home after taxes and deductions). Understanding net income is important because it reflects the actual funds available for budgeting.

Understanding expenses:

Expenditure includes all the money you spend to meet your needs, desires, and financial commitments. Categorizing your spending gives you insight into your spending behavior and helps you identify areas where you can potentially save or reduce costs. Here are some common expense categories.

Fixed cost:
These are recurring expenses that are relatively constant each month, such as: B. Rent or Mortgage Payments, Insurance Premiums, and Subscription Services.

Variable cost:
These expenses vary from month to month, such as groceries, utilities, transportation, and entertainment. It's important to consider the variability of these costs when creating your budget.

Discretionary expenses:
These fees are not mandatory and reflect your choices and preferences. Examples include dining out, hobbies, vacations, and entertainment. Discretionary spending brings more joy to life, but it's important to allocate the right portion of your income to it within your budget.

Tracking your spending is essential to fully understand where your money is being spent. Accurately track your spending with tools like spreadsheets, budgeting apps, and financial software. This allows you to identify areas where you may be overspending and adjust accordingly.

Understanding cash flow:

Cash flow is the flow of money into your account over a period of time (usually monthly). Maintaining positive cash flow, where income exceeds expenses, is important to ensure financial stability and avoid accumulating debt.

By analyzing your income and expenses, you can get an idea of your cash flow situation. Positive cash flow allows you to allocate funds for savings, investments, and debt repayment. Negative cash flow, on the other hand, indicates that you spend more than you earn, which can lead to financial difficulties and debt.

To improve your cash flow, focus on increasing your income or decreasing your expenses. Align cash flow with financial goals through effective budgeting and conscious spending decisions.

Diploma:

Understanding your income, expenses and cash flow is the foundation of effective budgeting. Getting clarity on these aspects will help you make informed decisions about how to spend your money, save for the future, and achieve financial security. A budget gives you the framework you need to prioritize your needs, track your spending, and adjust as needed. In the next section, we'll explore practical strategies for creating separate budgets to meet your financial goals.

Create A Personal Budget

Introduction:

This chapter details the process of creating a personal budget, a powerful tool to help you manage your finances and make conscious decisions about money. A personal budget serves as a roadmap to help you manage your income, expenses, and savings and reach your financial goals. By following the steps in this chapter, you can create a budget that reflects your priorities and helps build a strong financial foundation.

Step 1:
Determine your financial goals.

Before starting the budgeting process, it's important to determine your financial goals. What do you want to achieve with your money? Your goals may include saving for retirement, paying off debt, buying a home, starting a business, or educating your children. Understanding your goals can help you adjust your budget and make good financial decisions to meet your long-term goals.

Step 2:
Assess your current financial situation.

Creating an effective budget requires a clear picture of your current financial situation. First, collect all relevant financial documents, including bank statements, credit card statements, pay stubs, and other sources of income and expenditure. Calculate your total income, review your spending over the past few months, and identify trends and areas where you may be spending too much.

Step 3:
Categorize your spending.

Categorizing your spending is an important step in budgeting. This allows you to understand where your money is being spent and identify areas where you may be able to reduce or optimize your spending. Common spending categories include housing, transportation, utilities, groceries, entertainment, debt service, insurance, and savings. We customize our categories to your specific situation to ensure that all costs are covered precisely.

Step 4:
Set realistic budget goals.

Set realistic budget targets based on your financial goals and assessment of your current situation. Start by assigning a percentage of your income to each expense category. Essential spending like housing, utilities, and debt repayments should be prioritized, while discretionary spending can be adjusted based on financial priorities. Set aside a portion of your income for savings or an emergency fund. Remember to keep your goals realistic and flexible so that they stay within your budget in the long run.

Step 5:

Track and monitor your budget.

Creating a budget is not a one-time activity. Requires consistent tracking and monitoring. Regularly track your income, expenses, and savings using a personal finance app, spreadsheet, or budgeting software. Monitor progress and adjust as needed to stay within the budgets assigned to each spending category. Reviewing your budget on a regular basis will help you identify opportunities for improvement and keep you on track to meet your financial goals.

Step 6:
Adjust and adapt.

Life is full of change and you need to be able to adjust your budget accordingly. Be prepared to adjust your budget accordingly if circumstances change, such as changes in income, new expenses, or unexpected events. Flexibility is key to maintaining a sustainable budget that meets your financial goals.

Diploma:

Creating a personal budget is an important step in mastering finance. By following the steps outlined in this chapter, you will be able to create a budget that reflects your financial goals and make informed decisions about money. Remember that budgeting is a dynamic process that requires regular review and adjustment. The next section explores savings and investment strategies that further improve financial well-being.

Track And Manage Expenses Effectively

Introduction:

This chapter examines the importance of effectively tracking and controlling your spending. Tracking your spending gives you a clear picture of where your money is being spent, identifies opportunities for improvement, and makes informed decisions about your spending. By implementing an effective spend management strategy, you can optimize your budget, save money, and work towards meeting your financial goals. Let's take a look at the essential steps for tracking and controlling your spending.

Step 1:
Collect expense information.

To effectively track your expenses, collect all relevant financial documents such as bank statements, credit card statements, receipts, and other expense records. See a summary of your spending over a period of time (usually 1 or 3 months) to get a realistic picture of your spending habits.

Step 2:
Categorize your spending.

Categorizing expenses is an important step in tracking expenses. Create categories that match your spending habits and financial goals. Common spending categories include housing, transportation, groceries, dining out, entertainment, utilities, subscriptions, debt repayments, and savings. Compare each expense to its respective category to get a clear picture of how your money is allocated.

Step 3:
Select an expense tracking method.

Choose the expense tracking method that works best for you. You can use traditional methods such as pen and paper, or create a spreadsheet to manually record your expenses. Alternatively, you can use digital tools such as budgeting apps and personal finance software that automate the tracking process. Choose the method that ensures accuracy and convenience that suits your taste.

Step 4:
Understand and analyze your spending.

Consistently track your spending by entering your spending into the tracking system of your choice. Be careful when recording both small and large expenses. Review your expense reports regularly and analyze your spending behavior. Identify areas where you may be overspending, or where you could cut back to free up more money for savings or other financial goals.

Step 5:
Set budget limits for each category.

Set budget limits for each spending category based on your analysis. Determine how much you are willing to spend in each category based on your financial goals and priorities. Setting limits helps you control your spending and make sure it's aligned with your income and overall budget.

Step 6:
Check and adjust regularly.

Regularly review expense tracking records and compare against budget limits. Evaluate progress and make adjustments as needed. If you are consistently over budget in certain categories, consider strategies to cut back on those spending or reallocate funds from other categories. Keep in mind that tracking and managing expenses is an ongoing process that requires regular evaluation and adjustment.

Step 7:
Use expense management tools.

Simplify and improve expense management with technology and personal finance tools. Find a budgeting app that automatically syncs with your bank account and categorizes your spending. These tools often provide a visual view of your spending, making it easier to spot trends and areas for improvement.

Diploma:

Effectively tracking and managing your spending is a key component of building a strong financial foundation. By taking the steps described in this chapter, you can control your spending, optimize your budget, and work towards your financial goals. Tracking your spending regularly and making informed decisions about spending leads to greater financial awareness and stability. The following sections explore the concept of saving and investing, offering strategies for growing wealth and securing your financial future.

Practical Tips For Saving Money

Introduction:

In this chapter, we'll look at practical money-saving tips and strategies that are essential for building a strong financial foundation. By saving money, you can prepare an emergency fund, meet your financial goals, and secure your future. By following these tips, you can develop effective saving habits and get your money spent on yourself. Let's take a look at some practical money-saving tips.

Tip 1:
Create a budget and stick to it.

A budget serves as your financial roadmap, helping you allocate your income to spending, savings, and goals. Create a budget that allows you to meet your financial goals and set aside some of your income for savings. Stay on budget by tracking your spending, avoiding unnecessary purchases, and making conscious spending decisions.

Tip 2:
Automate your savings.

Automating your savings is a powerful technique to combat the temptation to spend the money you want to save. Set up automatic transfers from your checking account to another savings or investment account at regular intervals, preferably right after you receive your paycheck. In this way, you can keep saving continuously without relying solely on your own will.

Tip 3:
Reduce unnecessary spending.

Cut back on unnecessary spending and identify areas where that money can be put into savings. Review your spending habits and look for ways to cut costs. Consider negotiating your bill, eating out less, canceling unused subscriptions, and finding cheaper alternatives without sacrificing quality.

Tip 4:
Set a savings goal.

Setting a specific savings goal can help motivate you to have a clear goal and continue to save. Determine short-term and long-term financial goals. For example, you can build an emergency fund, save for a down payment on a home, or fund your retirement. Break your goals down into achievable milestones and track your progress regularly.

Tip 5:
Track and analyze save progress.

Track and analyze your savings progress regularly to make sure you're on track to reach your goals. Monitor your savings and measure your progress against your goals with personal finance apps and spreadsheets. Analyze your savings behavior and identify opportunities for improvement. Celebrate milestones along the way to stay motivated.

Tip 6:
Develop cost-saving habits.

Incorporate cost-saving habits into your daily life. Check discounts, coupons and special offers before you buy. Compare great costs and negotiate prices if possible. Reduce your utility bills by practicing energy efficiency. Cook at home instead of eating out frequently. Small savings can add up significantly over time.

Tip 7:
Prioritize saving for luck or a raise.

You should consider making savings a priority when you have a lucky event such as a tax refund, bonus, or pay raise. While it may be tempting to spend more quickly, using some of the extra money to save will accelerate your progress and help you reach your financial goals sooner.

Diploma:

Practicing practical money-saving tips is an important step in building a solid financial foundation. Build strong savings habits by creating budgets, automating savings, cutting unnecessary expenses, setting savings goals, tracking progress, adopting cost-saving habits, and prioritizing savings. and achieve financial stability. Remember, every dollar you save brings you one step closer to financial freedom.

CHAPTER 3:

Savings and Emergency Funds

Section 1:
the importance of saving money

Saving money is a fundamental aspect of personal finance that lays the foundation for financial stability and success. This chapter examines different aspects of saving and how it contributes to overall financial well-being. A disciplined approach to saving can help you reach your financial goals and weather unexpected storms.

Section 2:
Distinguish between short-term and long-term savings goals

To save money effectively, it's important to understand the difference between short-term and long-term savings goals. Short-term goals are typically costs you expect to incur within the next 1-3 years. B. Buy a new car, take a vacation, or save for a down payment on a home. Long-term goals, on the other hand, include financial goals years or decades ahead, such as saving for retirement or funding your children's education. By distinguishing between these two types of goals, you can create a customized savings strategy tailored to your specific goals.

Section 3:
Build an emergency fund for unexpected expenses

Life is unpredictable and unexpected expenses can arise at any time. For this reason, building an emergency fund is important. An emergency fund acts as an economic safety net, providing a buffer against contingencies such as medical emergencies, unemployment, and major home renovations. In this section, we look at the importance of having an emergency fund, how much you should save, and strategies for building and maintaining an emergency fund. Having enough emergency funds can help you get through tough times without debt or financial stress.

Section 4:
Strategies for automating savings

One of the most effective ways to ensure consistent savings habits is to automate the process. Automating your savings allows you to save a portion of your income on a regular basis without requiring any conscious effort or willpower. Consider different strategies and tools to help automate savings, including: B. Direct Deposits to Another Savings Account, Automatic Transfers, or Use of Budgeting Apps. Practicing these techniques will help you establish a second habit, a savings routine, and help you reach your financial goals.

Diploma:

The path to mastering finance begins with understanding the importance of saving and having an emergency fund ready. By distinguishing between short-term and long-term savings goals, building a strong emergency fund, and automating your savings, you can ensure you're on the road to financial stability. The following chapters delve deeper into specific areas of personal finance, providing knowledge and strategies for controlling future economic conditions. Remember, every step you take to manage your money brings you closer to financial freedom and security.

The Importance Of Saving Money

Saving money is a fundamental aspect of personal finance that lays the foundation for financial stability and success. This lays the foundation for sound financial management and puts individuals in control of their financial future. In this chapter, we'll look at the importance of saving money and how it can positively impact your life in different ways.

Part 1:
MONEY SAVING BENEFITS

1.1. Build Financial Security:

Saving money builds a safety net for you and your loved ones. Provides a buffer against unexpected events such as job losses, medical emergencies, and unexpected expenses. Savings can help you get through tough times without going into debt or jeopardizing your long-term financial goals.

1.2. Achieve financial goals:

Whether it's buying a home, starting a business, or traveling the world, saving is essential to achieving your dreams. Saving helps you save the money you need to meet your financial goals, whether short or long term. Seize the opportunity and provide the necessary capital to launch a new business.

1.3. Accumulation of Wealth:

Saving money is not just about saving cash. It is also about building wealth over time. By saving a portion of your income on a regular basis, you can invest that savings to generate additional income and increase your net worth. When you save money, you can harness the power of compound interest to take advantage of investment opportunities that lead to long-term economic growth.

1.4. Gain Financial Independence:

Financial independence is a goal shared by many. As you save money, you gradually become less dependent on outside sources of income and gain more control over your financial destiny. Building up significant savings gives you the freedom to make decisions based on your values and priorities, whether it's a new career, starting a business, or retiring early.

Part 2:
Overcome the savings barrier

2.1. Overcome Procrastination:

One of the biggest obstacles to saving money is procrastination. Many people delay saving for a variety of reasons, such as thinking they don't have enough income or thinking they can start later. This section discusses strategies for overcoming procrastination and establishing saving habits that align with your financial goals.

2.2. Dealing with lifestyle inflation:

As your income increases, your expenses generally increase accordingly. This phenomenon, known as lifestyle inflation, can thwart your savings efforts. Consider strategies to manage lifestyle inflation and redirect some of your increased income toward savings and wealth building.

2.3. Change Attitudes and Behaviors:

Saving money requires changing the way you think and act. It's about making conscious spending decisions, prioritizing long-term goals over short-term gratification, and developing the habit of thrift. This section provides insights and practical tips to help you change your thinking and behavior so you can save more effectively.

Diploma:

Understanding the importance of saving money is the first step to financial empowerment. Saving money gives you the freedom to build financial security, reach your goals, accumulate wealth, and live life on your own terms. In the next sections of this book, we explore various strategies and techniques that can help you save effectively, distinguish between short-term and long-term savings goals, build an emergency fund, and automate your savings. Remember, every dollar you save puts you one step closer to financial independence and a more secure future.

Distinguish Between Short-Term And Long-Term Savings Goals

Saving money is not a panacea for everyone. It's about setting specific goals based on your financial wants and needs. This chapter takes a closer look at the importance of distinguishing between short-term and long-term savings goals. Understanding these differences will help you prioritize your financial goals and allocate resources effectively.

Part 1:

Define short-term savings goals

1.1. Immediate financial need:

Short-term savings goals are usually aimed at meeting immediate financial needs or anticipated expenses within the next 1-3 years. This includes saving for vacations, buying new appliances, paying off high-interest debt, paying a down payment on a car, and more.

1.2. Creation of an emergency fund:

Building an emergency fund is an important short-term savings goal. The fund acts as a financial safety net to cover unexpected expenses such as medical emergencies, home repairs and temporary unemployment. Later sections of this chapter discuss recommended sizes of emergency funds and strategies for building them.

1.3. Manage Seasonal Expenses:

Certain expenses are common, but not always unexpected. Examples include vacation expenses, property taxes, and annual insurance premiums. By identifying and planning for these expenses, you can avoid financial stress and maintain financial stability throughout the year.

Section 2:
Understand your long-term savings goals

2.1. Post-retirement planning:

One of the most important long-term savings goals is planning for retirement. Retirement savings can help ensure financial security during golden years, maintain the lifestyle you want, and cover necessary expenses. Later chapters will delve deeper into retirement planning and offer strategies for maximizing your savings and investment opportunities.

2.2. Education Funding:

Saving money on education is a long-term goal for those who have children or are looking to go on to higher education. Training costs can be significant. So, by starting your education funding early and contributing regularly to the education fund, you can reduce your student loan burden and provide a quality education to your loved ones.

2.3. Wealth Accumulation and Economic Independence:

Long-term savings goals also include building wealth and achieving financial independence. Building wealth through investments such as stocks, real estate, and entrepreneurship creates passive income streams that increase your net worth over time. Financial independence gives you more control over your life choices and allows you to pursue your passions without relying solely on traditional employment.

Section 3:
Balancing short-term and long-term goals

3.1. Prioritize your goals:

Balancing short-term and long-term savings goals requires careful prioritization. It is important to consider your current financial situation, assess your needs and wishes, and allocate resources accordingly. Prioritize goals and discuss strategies for finding the right balance between immediate needs and long-term financial security.

3.2. Periodic Reviews and Adjustments:

It's important to regularly review and adjust your savings goals as your life circumstances change. What was once a short-term goal may turn into a long-term goal, and vice versa. Regular evaluations and adjustments will help you stay on track and adapt your savings plan to changing financial conditions.

Diploma:

Distinguishing between short-term and long-term savings goals is essential for effective financial planning. Understanding this difference can help you prioritize your financial goals, allocate resources wisely, and create a roadmap for achieving both short-term financial needs and long-term financial security. In the next chapter, we'll dive deeper into specific strategies for saving, budgeting, and investing, giving you the knowledge and tools to master your money and reach your financial goals. Remember: A balanced savings plan lays the foundation for a successful future.

Build An Emergency Fund For Unexpected Expenses

An emergency fund is an integral part of a strong financial base. Life is unpredictable and unexpected expenses can arise at any time, leading to financial stress and instability. In this chapter, we look at the importance of building an emergency fund, how much you should save, and strategies for building and maintaining that financial safety net.

Part 1:
The Importance of Emergency Funds

1.1. Financial stability and security:

An emergency fund gives you a sense of security and peace of mind. It acts as a buffer, protecting you from unforeseen financial hardships such as medical emergencies, car repairs, or sudden job losses. Adequate emergency funds can meet these challenges without resorting to high-interest debt or jeopardizing long-term economic goals.

1.2. To avoid the debt trap:

Without an emergency fund, unexpected expenses can quickly add to your debt. Relying on credit cards and loans for emergencies can create cycles of debt and interest payments that can threaten your financial health. Having an emergency fund reduces your reliance on debt by allowing you to cover unexpected expenses with your own funds.

1.3. Maintain financial progress:

Building an emergency fund can help you maintain progress toward your financial goals. Without them, a single unforeseen event can ruin your plans and deplete your savings and investments. An emergency fund protects your hard-earned money and ensures that you stay on track and keep moving forward.

Section 2:
Determine the size of your emergency fund

2.1. Evaluate your spending.

To determine the size of your emergency fund, first assess your monthly expenses. Consider essential expenses such as housing, utilities, groceries, transportation, and debt payments. Save at least 3-6 months of these expenses so you can adequately manage the unexpected.

2.2. Considering your personal situation:

Your personal circumstances can affect the size of your emergency fund. Factors such as job stability, health status, and dependents should be considered. If you are at high risk of losing your job or have large financial commitments, it is wise to aim for a larger reserve fund.

2.3. Step-by-step savings approach:

Building an emergency fund can be a daunting task, especially when starting from scratch. Taking a step-by-step savings approach makes dealing with the problem easier. Set small achievable goals and regularly donate a portion of your income to an emergency fund. Over time, the funds will grow and provide greater financial security.

Section 3:
Strategies for building and managing emergency funds

3.1. Dedicated account setup:

Create a separate savings account specifically for your emergency fund. This separation allows us to track progress more effectively without relying on funds for non-urgent purposes.

3.2. Automate savings:

Automate your savings by setting up automatic transfers from your checking account to your emergency fund. This will allow you to contribute regularly without relying on willpower or memory. Consistency is key to building a robust emergency fund.

3.3. Spend less and earn more:

To accelerate your emergency fund growth, consider reducing your discretionary spending or finding ways to increase your income. Review your budget, identify areas of savings, and explore additional revenue streams. Any extra dollars you save or earn can be donated to emergency funds.

Diploma:

Building an emergency fund is an important step toward financial stability and security. By building a solid and well-equipped safety net, you can protect yourself from unexpected expenses and avoid falling into the debt trap. Determine an appropriate emergency fund size based on your expenses and personal circumstances. Get into the habit of gradual savings and don't forget to automate your donations. In the next chapter, we'll dig deeper into your savings strategy and explore other ways you can maximize your financial potential. With a strong emergency fund, you'll be better prepared for life's unexpecteds and stay on track toward achieving your financial goals.

Strategies To Automate Savings

Automating your savings is a powerful technique that can help you build wealth consistently and effortlessly. Setting up a system that automatically puts a portion of your income into savings eliminates the need for constant decision-making and discipline. This chapter explores different strategies for automating savings and making it a seamless part of your financial routine.

Part 1:
pay yourself first

1.1. Prioritize savings:

A pay-for-yourself policy treats savings as a non-negotiable expense. As income is received, it allocates a predetermined percentage or amount directly to savings before using the funds for other expenses. By prioritizing savings, you can ensure your financial future is protected.

1.2. Set up direct deposit.

If your employer offers direct deposit, take advantage of this handy feature. Tell your employer to automatically deposit part of your salary into a separate savings account. This makes it easier to reach your savings goals by ensuring that your savings are allocated before you spend them.

Section 2:
automatic transfers and donations

2.1. Create a special savings account.

Set up special savings accounts for long-term goals or emergency funds. This separation makes it easier to track progress and avoid funds being spent on unnecessary spending. To get the most out of your savings, choose an account with competitive interest rates.

2.2. Set call forwarding.

To set up automatic transfers from your checking account to your savings account, contact your bank or financial institution. Determine the frequency to align with your financial goals. B. Weekly, bi-weekly, or monthly transfers. This automated process ensures consistent savings without the need for active effort. 2.3. Take advantage of your employer's pension plan.

If your employer offers a retirement plan such as her 401(k) or similar, make the most of it. Pay a percentage of your income, preferably up to your employer's contribution, into your retirement account. These contributions are automatically deducted from your paycheck so you don't have to constantly monitor them and can help you save for retirement.

Section 3:
Roundup App and Microsaves

3.1. Summary app:

Consider using a round-up app or service that rounds up your daily purchases to the nearest dollar and automatically deposits the difference into your savings or investment account. With this hassle-free method, you'll start saving money before you know it as your change will add up over time.

3.2. Microsaving apps:

Microsavings apps work by analyzing your spending patterns and automatically transferring small amounts from your checking account to your savings account or investment portfolio. These apps use technology to make saving easy and step-by-step, making saving a part of your daily life.

Diploma:

Automating your savings is a key factor in reaching your financial goals. By implementing strategies such as, for example, paying yourself first, setting up direct deposits, and using automatic transfers, saving becomes a consistent and easy part of your financial routine. Additionally, the Roundup and microsavings apps offer innovative ways to save without requiring any conscious effort. By leveraging these automated strategies, you can build wealth over time and make significant strides toward your financial goals.

CHAPTER 4:

Overview of Debt Management

This chapter looks at debt management, an essential aspect of achieving financial stability and freedom. Understanding different types of debt, implementing strategies for managing and reducing debt, considering debt consolidation and refinancing opportunities, and developing a debt free plan are important parts of this chapter. Mastering debt management gives you the tools you need to control your financial future.

Part 1:
Understanding Different Types of Debt
Debt comes in many forms, so it's important to understand the different types before implementing a debt management plan. We'll look at common types of debt such as credit card debt, student loans, mortgages, personal loans, and car loans. Understanding the characteristics, interest rates and potential risks associated with each type of debt provides a solid foundation for effective debt management.

Section 2:
Debt management and reduction strategies
Dealing with debt requires a proactive approach and the

implementation of effective strategies. This section provides practical techniques for managing debt responsibly. Topics include creating a budget, prioritizing debt repayment, negotiating with creditors, and using debt repayment methods such as snowball and avalanche. By implementing these strategies, you can take back control of your finances and make great strides in reducing your debt burden.

Section 3:

Debt consolidation and refinancing options

Debt consolidation and refinancing can be powerful tools that make it easier to pay off debt and potentially lower interest rates. This section explores various options for consolidating debt, including: B. Personal Loans, Balance Transfer Credit Cards, and Home Equity Loans. Additionally, we discuss the benefits and considerations of refinancing an existing loan to secure more favorable terms. Understanding these options can help you make informed decisions and streamline the debt settlement process.

Section 4:

Make a plan to get out of debt

Getting out of debt requires a clear plan and commitment to financial discipline. The final section of this chapter will guide you through the process of creating a comprehensive debt resolution plan. Consider steps such as setting clear financial goals, prioritizing debt, allocating resources effectively, and monitoring progress. A solid plan will motivate and prepare you for steady progress toward a debt-free future.

<u>Diploma</u>

<u>Debt management is a fundamental pillar of personal finance and this chapter provides a solid coverage of this important topic. Understanding the different types of debt, implementing effective debt management and reduction strategies, considering debt consolidation and refinancing options, and developing a debt</u>

free plan will help you get better control over your finances. Remember, with knowledge and perseverance, you can overcome debt and begin your journey to financial security and freedom.

Understanding Different Types Of Debt

Understanding the different types of debt is an important step in mastering finance. Debt can have a significant impact on your financial well-being. Understanding the different forms of this debt can help you make informed decisions about your personal finances. This chapter reviews the most common types of debt faced by individuals and discusses their characteristics, implications and potential risks. A thorough understanding of these types of debt can help you better navigate the complex world of personal finance.

Credit card debt:

Credit card debt is one of the most common forms of debt and can quickly accumulate if not managed responsibly. We'll explore how credit cards work, including the concept of interest rates, minimum payments, and the possible effects of high balances. We also share strategies for using credit cards responsibly and provide tips on how to effectively manage and reduce credit card debt.

Student loans:

Many people are aiming for higher education and rely on student loans to pay for their studies. To effectively manage this particular type of debt, it's important to understand the intricacies of student loans, including: B. Differences Between Federal and Personal Loans, Repayment Options, and Possible Waiver Programs. We dive into the world of student loans, giving you the knowledge to make informed decisions and develop repayment plans. Housing loan:

Mortgages play an important role in home purchases. We consider key factors for a mortgage, including interest rates, down payment, loan terms, and potential benefits of home ownership. Understanding your mortgage details can help you make informed decisions when choosing a mortgage, managing your payments, and even considering refinancing options.

Personal loan:

A personal loan can serve as a financial lifeline in case of an emergency or to finance an important purchase. However, it also comes with some considerations. Learn about the nature of personal loans, including interest rates, repayment terms, and potential risks. Additionally, we provide tips on how to assess your personal loan needs and how to manage the borrowing process responsibly.

Car loan:

Buying a car often requires taking out a car loan. We explore the world of auto loans, covering topics such as interest rates, loan terms, down payments, and pitfalls to avoid. Understanding the details of car loans can help you make informed decisions about buying a car and managing the debt that comes with it.

Diploma

Understanding the different types of debt and their unique characteristics can help you approach your personal finances with more confidence. With this knowledge, you can develop effective strategies to manage and reduce your debt, make informed credit decisions, and ultimately achieve financial stability.The next section of this chapter details debt management and reduction strategies, explores debt consolidation and refinancing options, and helps you create a debt free plan.

Debt Management And Reduction Strategies

Debt can be overwhelming, but with the right strategies, you can manage your financial situation and aim for debt-free living. This chapter reviews effective debt management and reduction strategies. By implementing these strategies, you can gain a sense of self-determination and make significant progress toward your financial goals. Let's take a look at some practical approaches to debt management.

Create a budget

Budgeting is a fundamental step in debt management. By tracking your income and expenses, you can get a clear picture of where your money is going and identify areas where you can cut spending. Dedicate a portion of your budget specifically to debt repayment so that you can continue to contribute to debt reduction.

Prioritize debt repayment:

If you have multiple debts, it's important to prioritize them strategically. Two common approaches to debt consolidation are snowball and avalanche. In a snowball, the smallest debts are paid off first, with the smallest payments made on other debts. As you settle each debt, move on to the next one and build momentum. Avalanche methods, on the other hand, focus on paying off the debt at the highest interest rate first, saving interest payments in the long run. Choose a method that fits your financial goals and motivate you to reach them.

Negotiate with creditors:

In some cases, it may be possible to negotiate a lower interest rate or a more manageable repayment schedule with the creditor. Contact your creditors and explain your financial situation. They may be more than happy to work with you to develop a repayment plan that is more suited to your current circumstances. By negotiating with your creditors, you can reduce the stress of high interest rates and create more room to pay off your debt.

Discover Debt Relief Programs:

Depending on your situation, you may be eligible for a debt consolidation assistance program. Offered by government agencies and non-profit organizations, these programs can help you manage your debt and provide advice. They may also offer counseling services, debt consolidation options, and even debt relief programs. Check out the programs available in your area to see if you meet the eligibility criteria and take advantage of the support they offer.

Increase your income:

Increasing your current income can speed up the road to paying off debt. Consider ways to increase your income, such as: B. Accept a part-time or freelance job. Consider using your skills and hobbies to generate additional income streams. The money you earn can be used to pay off your debts, so you can pay off your debts faster.

Diploma

Remember that managing and reducing debt is a step-by-step process that requires patience and discipline. Stick to your debt management plan, track progress regularly, and celebrate milestones along the way. By implementing these strategies and staying focused on your financial goals, you can make steady progress toward debt freedom.

The next section of this chapter explores debt consolidation and refinancing options to help you create a comprehensive debt free plan. With the right strategy and a clear roadmap, you can overcome debt and achieve financial freedom.

Debt Consolidation And Refinancing Options

Debt consolidation and refinancing can be valuable tools in your journey towards effective debt management. In this chapter, we will explore various options available for consolidating your debts and refinancing existing loans. These strategies can simplify your repayment process, potentially lower your interest rates, and provide a clearer path towards becoming debt-free. Let's delve into debt consolidation and refinancing options to help you optimize your debt management efforts.

Debt Consolidation:
Debt consolidation involves combining multiple debts into a single loan or credit account. This approach can simplify your repayment process by streamlining multiple payments into one monthly installment. Here are a few common methods of debt consolidation:

a.   *Personal Loans*: You can obtain a personal loan to pay off your high-interest debts, such as credit card balances or medical bills. By consolidating these debts into a personal loan, you can benefit from a potentially lower interest rate and a fixed repayment term.

b.   *Balance Transfer Credit Cards:* Some credit card companies offer balance transfer options that allow you to transfer your high-interest credit card debt onto a new card with a lower or zero introductory interest rate. This strategy can provide temporary relief from high-interest charges, enabling you to make more substantial debt repayments.

c.   ***Home Equity Loans or Lines of Credit***: If you own a home and have built up equity, you may qualify for a home equity loan or line of credit. These loans allow you to borrow against the value of your home and use the funds to pay off your debts. Home equity loans often come with favorable interest rates and longer repayment terms.

Debt consolidation and refinancing options

Debt consolidation and refinancing are valuable tools for effective debt management. In this chapter, we'll look at different ways to consolidate debt and refinance existing loans. These strategies simplify the repayment process, potentially lower interest rates, and give you a clearer path to debt freedom. Learn more about debt consolidation and refinancing options to streamline debt management.

Debt consolidation:

Debt consolidation is the process of consolidating multiple debts into a single loan or credit account. This approach simplifies the repayment process by consolidating multiple payments into one monthly installment. Common debt consolidation methods include:

A.   Personal loans:
You can take out a personal loan to pay off high-interest debt, such as credit card balances or medical bills. By consolidating this debt into a personal loan, you may be able to take advantage of lower interest rates and fixed repayment terms.

B.   Balance transfer credit card:
Some credit card companies offer balance transfer options that allow you to transfer your high-interest credit card debt to a new card with a lower or no interest rate. This strategy

provides a temporary relief from the high interest burden and an opportunity to pay off a large amount of debt.

C.   *Mortgage Loans or Lines of Credit:*

If you own a home and have accumulated assets, you may be eligible for a home equity loan or line of credit. With these loans, you can borrow the value of your home and use that money to pay off your debt. Home equity loans often have lower interest rates and longer repayment terms.

Before proceeding, it's important to consider the terms and costs associated with each integration option. Consider factors such as interest rates, fees, repayment terms, and potential impact on your credit score. Choose the option that meets your financial goals and offers the most favorable terms for your unique situation.

Refinancing:

Refinancing replaces an existing loan with a new loan with more favorable terms. This can be done for different types of loans such as mortgages, car loans, and personal loans. The main purpose of refinancing is to improve interest rates, reduce monthly payments, or extend the repayment period. Here are some common scenarios where refinancing is beneficial.

A.   *Mortgage refinancing:*

If interest rates have been dropping since you took out your mortgage, refinancing can lower your interest rate, reduce your monthly payments, and potentially save you money in the long run. Refinancing also allows you to switch from a variable rate mortgage to a fixed rate mortgage, which makes your monthly payments more stable. B. Auto Loan Refinancing:
If you have a high-interest auto loan, refinancing can lower your interest rate, reduce your monthly payments, and potentially save you money over the life of the loan. It is important to compare the offers of different financial institutions and consider the fees

associated with refinancing.

C. *Personal loan refinancing:*

If you have a personal loan with unfavorable terms, refinancing can be an opportunity to secure better terms, such as lower interest rates or longer repayment terms. This can help you manage your monthly payments better and save interest.

Carefully assess the costs and benefits involved before refinancing. Consider factors such as closing costs, upfront penalties, and overall financial impact. It is wise to seek professional advice or consult a financial advisor to determine if refinancing is the right choice for you.

Diploma

By looking at debt consolidation and refinancing options, you may be able to optimize your debt repayments, lower interest rates, and simplify your financial journey. However, it's important to keep in mind that these options are not a panacea. Assess your financial situation, compare terms and choose options that match your goals and financial capabilities.

The next section of this chapter will help you develop a comprehensive plan to get out of debt. A combination of effective debt management strategies, debt consolidation or refinancing options, and a well-defined plan puts you on track to achieving financial stability and freedom.

Make A Plan To Get Out Of Debt

Getting rid of debt is an encouraging goal that can greatly improve your financial well-being and pave the way to long-term financial stability. This chapter will help you develop a comprehensive plan to eliminate debt and achieve financial freedom. By following the steps outlined below, you can create a roadmap that will help you stay focused, motivated, and on track towards a debt-free future.

Evaluate your current debt situation.

First, take a closer look at your current debt situation. Create a list of all your debts, including balance, interest, and minimum monthly payments. This assessment provides a clear picture of the extent of the debt and serves as a starting point for the debt reduction plan.

Set clear and realistic goals.

Define your debt free goals by setting clear and realistic goals. Consider how long you want to reduce your debt and what specific milestones you want to achieve along the way. Setting measurable goals helps you stay motivated and track your progress.

Create a budget

Budgeting is an important part of any debt consolidation plan. Analyze your income and expenses to determine how much you can spend on your monthly debt payments. Be sure to consider essential expenses such as housing, utilities, and groceries, and identify areas where you can reduce discretionary spending to free up additional funds to pay off debt.

Execute a debt repayment strategy.

Choose a debt consolidation strategy that fits your goals and preferences. Two common methods are the snowball and avalanche methods described in this chapter. Whatever approach you take, be consistent and focus on paying off your debts regularly, one at a time until you're completely paid off.

Look for additional income opportunities.

Consider ways to increase your income to pay off debt faster. Look for side jobs, freelancers, and part-time jobs that match your skills and interests. The extra money you earn can have a big impact on paying off your debt faster.

Track your progress.

Check your progress regularly and celebrate milestones along the way. Visualize your progress and stay motivated with tools like debt tracking spreadsheets and mobile apps. As debt falls and financial freedom comes closer and closer, there will be increased commitment to debt reduction plans.

Stay motivated and stay disciplined.

Getting out of debt takes discipline and patience. Keep yourself motivated by remembering these benefits of being debt free: B. Less stress, more financial flexibility, and the opportunity to spend money for financial goals. Surround yourself with a supportive network of friends and family who encourage you and hold you accountable.

Seek professional help if necessary.

If you feel overwhelmed or are slow to make progress, don't be afraid to seek professional help. Financial advisors and credit bureaus provide professional advice tailored to your specific circumstances. They propose strategies, negotiate with creditors, and help develop more structured and achievable debt reduction plans.

Diploma

By developing a clear plan to get out of debt and sticking to your goals, you can regain control of your finances for the future. This path may take time and effort, but the feeling of freedom and peace of mind that comes from being debt free is priceless.

CHAPTER 5:

Basic investment principles

Introduction to investment

Investing is a fundamental aspect of personal finance that enables individuals to grow their wealth and reach their financial goals. This chapter serves as an introduction to the basic principles of investing, giving the reader a solid understanding of key concepts and strategies.

Various investment vehicles

In the investment world, a wide range of investment vehicles are available to individuals. This section reviews some of the most popular investment options such as stocks, bonds and mutual funds. We discuss each investment vehicle in detail, highlighting its features, benefits and potential risks. Familiarizing yourself with these different options will help you make informed investment decisions to reach your financial goals.

Risk tolerance and diversification

Knowing your risk tolerance is important when investing. This section explains the concept of risk and the relationship between risk and potential return. Readers will learn how to assess their risk tolerance and develop an investment strategy that matches their comfort level. Furthermore, this chapter emphasizes the importance of diversification to reduce investment risk. Learn how diversifying your investment portfolio across different asset classes and sectors can help mitigate potential losses and optimize long-term gains.

Long term investment strategy

Investing is a long-term commitment, and this section will focus on strategies and principles that can help you achieve your long-term financial goals. Readers will gain insight into the power of compound interest, the benefits of a disciplined investment approach, and the importance of realistic expectations. The chapter also emphasizes the importance of monitoring and adjusting investment portfolios as financial conditions change.

Diploma

> By the end of this chapter, the reader will have a solid foundation in basic investment principles. They have the knowledge necessary to make informed investment decisions, understand the potential risks and rewards of various investment vehicles, and develop long-term investment strategies aligned with financial goals. .

Remember that mastering the principles of investing takes time and practice. The purpose of this chapter is to provide a good starting point. However, it is important to keep expanding your knowledge and seek professional advice when needed. Dive into the exciting world of investing and start your journey to financial growth and prosperity.

Introduction To Investment

Investing is a key component of personal finance that enables individuals to grow their wealth and secure their financial future. This chapter serves as an introduction to basic investment principles, giving readers a solid understanding of the fundamentals and preparing them for more advanced investment strategies.

Investment definition

Investing can be defined as the process of allocating funds and resources with the expectation of yielding returns or benefits over time. This includes spending money to buy assets that have the potential to appreciate or generate income.

Why invest? Investing offers many benefits that help individuals achieve their financial goals. The main reasons to invest are:

Wealth Accumulation:
Investing provides an opportunity to grow wealth beyond traditional savings and checking accounts. You can grow your money over time by harnessing the power of compound interest.

Overcome Inflation:
Inflation erodes the purchasing power of money. The purpose of investing is to generate a return that exceeds the inflation rate and preserve the value of the asset. Achieve your financial goals:
Whether you're saving for retirement, buying a home, financing your education, or starting a business, investing can help you reach your long-term financial goals.

Build Passive Income:
Certain investments, such as rental properties and dividend-paying stocks, generate regular income and provide a passive source of income.

Risk and reward

Investing always involves risk. Understanding and managing risk is critical to making informed investment decisions. In general, investments with higher return potential come with higher risk. It is important to assess your own risk tolerance and understand that higher risk investments are subject to greater volatility and possible losses.

Diversification

Diversification is a strategy that reduces risk when investing. By diversifying your investments across different asset classes, sectors and geographies, you can reduce the impact of each investment on your overall portfolio. Diversification helps protect against unexpected market volatility and increases the chances of generating consistent profits over the long term.

Investment period

Investment period refers to the period of time you plan to hold your investment before you need to access the fund. Different investment goals have different time horizons. B. Short-term goals (1-3 years), medium-term goals (3-10 years), and long-term goals (10+ years). Investment horizons play an important role in determining the appropriate investment strategy and asset allocation for a portfolio.

Diploma

This section provides an overview of investments and emphasizes their importance to achieving financial goals and building wealth over time. Understanding the basics of investing, such as risk and reward, diversification, and investment horizons, will provide a solid foundation for exploring more advanced investment strategies that will be covered in the next chapter. Now let's take a closer look at various investment tools and how they can help you reach your financial goals.

Risk Tolerance And Diversification

When it comes to investing, understanding your risk tolerance and implementing a diversification strategy are key to building a resilient and balanced investment portfolio. This section discusses the concepts of risk tolerance and diversification and their importance to successful investing.

Risk tolerance

Risk tolerance is the willingness and ability to tolerate fluctuations in the value of an investment. It is influenced by factors such as your financial goals, time horizon, investment skills, and personal comfort level with uncertainty. It is important to assess your risk tolerance before making any investment decision to ensure that your investment strategy is consistent with your personal circumstances and goals.

To determine your risk tolerance, ask yourself the following questions:

What is the time horizon for this investment? Short term goals may require lower risk investments, while longer term goals may allow for higher risk investments.

How would you react to a significant drop in the value of your investment? Can short-term volatility be tolerated in exchange for potential long-term gains?

What is my overall financial situation? Factors such as income stability, debt levels and emergency funds can affect risk tolerance.

Understanding your own risk tolerance can help you make investment decisions that offer the best balance between potential return and acceptable level of risk. It is important to note that risk tolerance is subjective and may change over time as financial conditions and investment objectives change.

Diversification

Diversification is the strategy of spreading investments across different asset classes, sectors and geographies. The goal is to reduce the impact of any single investment on the overall portfolio. Diversification helps reduce risk by not putting all your eggs in one basket. Important aspects to consider regarding diversification are:

Asset class:

Divide your investments into different asset classes such as stocks, bonds, real estate, and commodities. Each asset class has its own risk and reward characteristics and its performance may vary depending on market conditions.

Sectors and Industries:

Further diversify within each asset class by investing in different sectors or industries. This helps mitigate the impact of economic downturns in specific sectors on the portfolio as a whole. Geographic Region:
Invest in companies and assets in different geographical regions. This diversifies our exposure to country-specific risks and provides access to potential growth opportunities in various markets.

Investment products:

Diversify your investment vehicle by exploring a mix of individual stocks, bonds, mutual funds, ETFs and other products. This ensures that investments are not overly focused on his one type of investment.

Diversification does not guarantee profits or prevent losses, but it does help manage risk and increase the likelihood of consistent profits over time. Monitor and rebalance your portfolio regularly to maintain diversification as different assets may perform differently.

<u>Diploma</u>

<u>Understanding your risk tolerance and implementing a diversification strategy are key ingredients to successful investing. Assessing your own risk tolerance can help you align your investment decisions with your financial goals and comfort level. Diversification reduces risk by spreading investments across different asset classes, sectors and geographies. The combination of risk tolerance and diversification provides a solid foundation for building a balanced investment portfolio that has the potential to withstand market volatility and generate long-term wealth. The next section discusses long-term investment strategies that can help you reach your financial goals.</u>

Various Investment Vehicles

The investment world has a wide variety of investment vehicles available to individuals, each with their own characteristics and potential benefits. This section aims to provide an overview of the most common investment options, including stocks, bonds, mutual funds, and more.

Stock

Shares, also known as stocks or stocks, represent ownership of a company. When you invest in a stock, you become a shareholder and get a return depending on the performance of the company. Stocks have the potential to appreciate as well as dividends, which are a portion of the company's profits distributed to shareholders. Investing in individual stocks requires research and analysis to identify growth potential and proven companies.

Knead

Bonds are bonds issued by governments, municipalities, or

corporations to raise capital. When you buy a bond, you're essentially lending money to the issuer in exchange for periodic interest payments and the return of principal at maturity. Bonds are generally considered to be a less risky and stable source of income than stocks. They differ in terms of credit quality, maturity and interest rate, offering options to suit different risk appetites and investment objectives.

Investment trust

A mutual fund pools the money of multiple investors to invest in a diverse portfolio of securities such as stocks, bonds, or both. These are managed by professional fund managers who make investment decisions on behalf of investors. Mutual funds hold a variety of assets and can provide instant diversification. It is available in various categories such as stock funds, bond funds, index funds and industry funds. Investors can choose funds based on their risk tolerance, investment goals and time horizon.

Exchange Traded Funds (ETFs)

ETFs are similar to mutual funds, but they trade on exchanges like individual stocks. They represent a basket of securities intended to track the performance of a particular index, sector, or asset class. ETFs are popular with investors due to their diversity, liquidity and flexibility. You can buy and sell at market prices throughout the trading day. ETFs provide access to a variety of markets and investment strategies, including Equity ETFs, Fixed Income ETFs, Commodity ETFs, and more.

Real estate investment trust (REIT)

A REIT is an investment vehicle that owns and manages income-producing properties such as commercial buildings, apartments, and shopping malls. Investing in REITs gives individuals access to the real estate market without owning the property directly. REITs provide regular income through rental payments and potential capital appreciation. These offer opportunities to diversify your investment portfolio and benefit from developments in the real estate sector.

Raw materials

Commodities include physical goods such as gold, silver, oil, natural gas and agricultural products. Investing in commodities can be done in a variety of ways, including commodity futures contracts, commodity-specific mutual funds and ETFs, and direct purchases of physical commodities. Commodities act as an inflation hedge and provide diversification. However, it also comes with inherent risks such as price fluctuations and storage costs.

Diploma

Understanding different investment vehicles is essential to building a balanced investment portfolio. Each investment option carries its own risks, potential returns and suitability for particular investment objectives. Learn about stocks, bonds, mutual funds, ETFs, REITs and commodities so you can make informed decisions based on your risk tolerance, financial goals and investment preferences. The following sections discuss risk tolerance and diversification strategies to help you create a personalized investment approach to meet your financial goals.

Long Term Investment Strategy

Long-term investing is a powerful approach to building wealth and achieving financial goals. This section discusses key long-term investment principles and strategies that will help you get the most out of your investments and maximize potential returns over the long term.

Set clear financial goals

Before embarking on a long-term investment, it is important to set clear financial goals. Identify what you want to achieve in the long term. B. Retirement benefits, children's education funds, or home purchase funds. Setting specific, measurable, achievable, relevant, and time-bound (SMART) goals will give you direction and help you make investment decisions.

Harness the Power of Compound Interest

Compound interest is an important concept in long-term investing. This refers to the ability of an investment to generate income, which can be reinvested to generate further income. Over time, the compounding effect can significantly increase your investment return. The sooner you start investing and the longer you keep investing, the greater the compounding effect.

Adopt a buy-and-hold approach

Long-term investing often involves employing a buy-and-hold strategy to invest in high-quality assets with high growth potential and hold them for the long term. This approach avoids unnecessary transaction costs and transaction costs, allowing you to benefit from increased long-term value of your investments. It is important to conduct thorough research and select investments with solid track records, growth prospects and good long-term prospects.

Average dollar cost

Dollar cost averaging is the strategy of investing a fixed amount of money on a regular basis, regardless of the price of the asset. If you invest consistently over time, you will buy more stocks when prices are low and more stocks when prices are high. This approach helps smooth out the effects of market volatility and reduces the risk of making poor investment decisions due to short-term market volatility. Stay up to date and check out our portfolio

Even with long-term investment strategies, it is important to stay informed about investment performance and review your portfolio regularly. Monitor economic trends, industry developments and changes in investment objectives. Regularly rebalancing the balance of your portfolio helps you maintain proper asset allocation and ensure that it aligns with your risk tolerance and long-term goals.

Be patient and be disciplined

Long-term investing requires patience and discipline. Market volatility and short-term fluctuations are inevitable, but staying focused on your long-term goals will help you get through these times. Do not impulsively make investment decisions based on short-term market movements. Take a long-term view and remember that investing success is a marathon, not a sprint.

Diploma

A long-term investment strategy can help you grow your wealth over the long term and reach your financial goals. Navigating market ups and downs by setting clear goals, leveraging the power of compound interest, adopting a buy-and-hold approach, practicing dollar-cost averaging, staying informed, and showing patience and discipline , you can maximize your potential. investment. Remember that investing is a long-term journey. Staying true to your strategy while adapting to changing conditions increases your chances of financial success.

CHAPTER 6:

Retirement plan overview

Introduction:

Retirement planning is an important aspect of personal finance management, but it is often neglected until later in life. But it's never too early to start preparing for retirement. This chapter discusses the importance of retirement savings, different retirement accounts such as 401(k)s and IRAs, strategies for maximizing your retirement savings, and decisions you need to make about Social Security and pensions. This section explains. Understanding these concepts and taking proactive steps can lay a solid foundation for a financially secure and fulfilling retirement.

Part 1:
Understand the importance of retirement planning
Retirement is the stage in life when people move from being an active income earner to being dependent on accumulated savings and investments. It's important to plan ahead and set retirement goals to maintain the lifestyle you want, pursue new hobbies and interests, and have the financial freedom to enjoy your golden years. Poor planning can make it difficult to manage your finances and compromise your quality of life in retirement.

Section 2:
Various retirement accounts (401(k), IRA, etc.)
There are a variety of retirement accounts available to individuals, each with their own benefits and merits. Two common types are 401(k) plans and individual retirement accounts (IRAs). A 401(k)

is an employer-provided retirement account that allows you to contribute a portion of your pre-tax income and may benefit from your employer's contributions. An IRA, on the other hand, is an individual retirement account that provides tax benefits to people who are not eligible for a plan offered by their employer. Learn more about these accounts, including contribution limits, eligibility criteria, and related tax implications.

Section 3:

Strategies for maximizing retirement savings
To maximize your retirement savings, you need to use smart strategies to make the most of your available resources. We will discuss some key strategies such as: These include starting early to take advantage of the power of compound interest, setting realistic savings goals, diversifying your investment portfolio, and regularly reviewing and adjusting your retirement plans as needed. It is included. Additionally, we explore the concept of asset allocation and how it can help balance risk and return in retirement portfolios.

Section 4:

Decisions on Social Security and Pensions
Social security and pensions are important components of retirement income for many people. Understanding how these programs work and what decisions you need to make are critical to an effective retirement plan. Learn more about Social Security, including eligibility requirements, application strategies, and how to get the most out of your benefits. It also discusses annuities and considerations when deciding between lump sum and monthly annuities.

Diploma:

Proper retirement planning is fundamental to personal finances and ensures a financially secure and comfortable future. Understanding the importance of retirement planning, familiarizing yourself with different retirement accounts, implementing effective savings strategies, and making informed Social Security and pension decisions will help you achieve a fulfilling, worry-free retirement. can walk the path of This chapter provides you with the knowledge and tools you need to make confident retirement decisions and achieve long-term financial stability.

The Importance Of Retirement Plans

Retirement planning is an important aspect of personal finance management and requires careful consideration and proactive decision-making. This chapter delves into the importance of retirement planning and highlights the key elements you need to understand. By preparing for early retirement and recognizing the importance of implementing effective strategies, you can ensure a comfortable and financially secure future.

Understand the importance of retirement planning:

Retirement is a stage in life when people transition from working years to a period of financial independence and relaxation. Understanding the importance of planning for retirement is crucial because it allows you to maintain the lifestyle you want, pursue your passions, and ensure your long-term financial security. Here are some reasons why planning for retirement is essential:

Alternative income:

A retirement plan ensures that you have enough money to replace your regular income when you stop working. By predicting future expenses and saving accordingly, you can close the income gap and maintain your standard of living.

Time axis:

The time to retirement can span decades, and planning for this long term is important. The sooner you start saving and investing, the longer it will take for your money to grow with compounding interest, and the bigger your retirement savings can be.

Inflation and Rising Costs:

Over time, inflation tends to increase the cost of living. Retirement planning can help you account for these increasing costs and ensure you have enough savings and investments to meet your future needs.

Independence and Peace of Mind:

With the right retirement plan, you can become financially independent and enjoy your retirement without worrying about constant financial problems. So you can focus on pursuing your passions, spending time with the people you love, and discovering new experiences.

By understanding the importance of retirement planning and the long-term benefits it can bring, you can take the necessary steps to ensure a comfortable and fulfilling retirement.

Diploma:

Retirement planning is an important aspect of personal finance management and should not be overlooked. Recognizing the importance of preparing for early retirement and understanding the factors involved will put you in control of your financial future. This chapter emphasized the importance of planning for retirement, replacing income, considering duration, considering inflation and rising costs, and stressing the need to aim for financial independence and peace of mind. With this understanding, you can start planning for your retirement and prepare yourself for a financially secure and comfortable retirement.

Various Retirement Accounts

Planning for retirement isn't just about saving money for the future, it's also about understanding the different retirement accounts available. This chapter covers various retirement accounts such as 401(k)s, IRAs, etc. Familiarizing yourself with these accounts and their unique features will help you make informed decisions based on your retirement goals and financial situation.

Various retirement accounts (401(k), IRA, etc.):

When it comes to retirement planning, it's important to understand the different types of retirement accounts. Here are some popular retirement accounts.

401(k) plans:
A 401(k) is an employer-initiated retirement plan that allows employees to contribute a portion of their pre-tax salary. These contributions are tax deferred and increase until they are withdrawn at retirement. Many employers also offer matching contributions, virtually free money to supplement your retirement savings. To maximize the benefits of your 401(k) plan, it's important to leverage your employer's contributions.

Traditional IRAs:
An Individual Retirement Account (IRA) is an individual retirement account that can be set up independently by an

individual. A traditional IRA allows you to make tax-deductible contributions up to certain limits based on your income. A traditional IRA's income is increased by deferring taxes and paying taxes on retirement withdrawals.

Ross IRA:

A Roth IRA is another type of personal retirement account. Donations to the Roth IRA are made in after-tax dollars. This means that they are not tax deductible. However, the advantage of a Roth IRA is that eligible withdrawals, both contributions and income, are tax-free upon retirement. A Roth IRA is especially beneficial if you anticipate higher taxes in the future. Simplified Employees' Pension (SEP) IRA:

A SEP IRA is a retirement account for self-employed or small business owners. Contributions to your SEP IRA are tax deductible and will increase your income for tax purposes until paid. SEP IRAs have higher contribution limits than traditional IRAs and Roth IRAs, which is advantageous for those with large self-employed income.

Solo 401(k) Plan:

Solo 401(k) plans, also known as individual 401(k) plans, are designed for self-employed people who have no employees other than their spouse. These plans offer similar benefits to his traditional 401(k) plans, including tax-deductible contributions and employer matching opportunities. Solo 401(k) plans also offer higher contribution limits, making them an attractive option for self-employed individuals looking to maximize their retirement savings.

Other Retirement Accounts:

In addition to the accounts above, other retirement options are available, including government and non-profit specific plans such as 403(b) and 457(b) plans, and self-governing IRAs that give you more control over your investment decisions. increase.

When choosing the right retirement account for your needs,

it's important to consider eligibility, contribution limits, tax implications, and employer offers.

Diploma:

Understanding the various retirement accounts, including 401(k)s, IRAs, and other options, is critical to effective retirement planning. Each account type has its own benefits, contribution limits, and tax implications. A good understanding of these options can help you make informed decisions to reach your financial goals. This chapter provides an overview of different retirement accounts, giving you the opportunity to choose the one that best suits your needs and pave the way to a secure and fulfilling retirement.

Make The Most Of Your Retirement Savings

Saving for retirement is not only about choosing the right retirement account, but also implementing effective strategies to maximize your savings. This chapter explores various strategies that can help you increase your retirement savings and build a solid financial foundation for your future. Understanding and implementing these strategies can optimize your retirement planning and increase your chances of achieving your retirement goals.

Strategies to maximize your retirement savings:

Start early and reap the benefits of compound interest:

One of the most effective strategies for maximizing your retirement savings is to start early. The sooner you start saving, the longer it will take for your money to grow thanks to the magic of compound interest. Compound interest ensures that investment returns generate additional returns over time. By starting early, even small contributions can accumulate significantly over decades.

Set realistic savings goals.

Setting realistic savings goals is very important in planning for retirement. Calculate how much money you'll need in retirement by considering your desired lifestyle, expected expenses, and expected medical expenses. Once you have your retirement savings goal in mind, you can work backwards to determine how much you'll need to save each month or year to reach that goal. Employer Matching Contribution Benefits:

If your employer offers a contributory retirement plan, make the most of it. Employer matching is basically free money and can significantly increase your retirement savings. This is a valuable opportunity to accelerate your retirement planning, so contribute at least enough to receive the maximum matching contribution from your employer.

Diversify your investments.

Diversification is an essential strategy to reduce risk and maximize profits. Rather than putting all his retirement savings in one investment, he diversifies his portfolio across different asset classes such as stocks, bonds, and real estate. This diversification helps reduce the impact of market volatility and increases long-term growth potential.

Regularly review and adjust your retirement plan.

Retirement plans should not be clearly defined. Review the plan regularly and adjust as necessary. Rethink your savings goals, investment outcomes, and living situation to ensure your retirement savings are in line with your current situation and goals. Consider talking to a financial advisor to help you make informed decisions and stay on track with your retirement savings. Add more posts over time.

If your income increases or your salary increases, you should consider increasing your pension premium. Allocating part of your salary to retirement is an effective way to continuously build your nest. Auto Contribution simplifies this process by automatically directing a percentage of your income to your retirement account.

Benefits of a catch-up donation:

When you turn 50, you become eligible for additional contributions to certain retirement accounts. Catch-up contributions allow you to contribute additional funds beyond your standard contribution limit to make up for lost time or accelerate your savings as you approach retirement.

Diploma

Maximizing your retirement savings requires a combination of discipline, informed decision-making, and strategic planning. Start early, take advantage of compound interest, set realistic goals, take advantage of employer contributions, diversify your investments, review your retirement plan regularly, increase contributions over time, catch You can increase your retirement savings potential by taking advantage of the Up Contribution. By implementing these strategies, you can ensure that you have a financially secure and comfortable retirement and enjoy your golden years with peace of mind.

Decisions On Social Security And Pensions

Retirement provisions are more than a savings and investment strategy. This includes making informed decisions about social security and pensions. This chapter reviews the considerations and decisions faced in relation to social security benefits and pensions. By understanding these decisions and how they will affect your retirement income, you can make informed decisions to reach your financial goals and get the most out of your retirement funds. can do.

Decisions on social security and pensions:

Understanding Social Security Benefits:

Social Security is a federal program designed to provide income for retirees. Understanding how social security benefits work is important to making informed decisions. Familiarize yourself with the factors that affect the level of performance, such as: B. Your income history, the age at which you would like to start receiving benefits, and the impact of early or late retirement.

Determining When to Claim Social Security Benefits:

An important decision related to Social Security is deciding when to start receiving benefits. You can claim benefits as early as age 62, but your monthly benefit amount is permanent compared to waiting until full retirement age (usually between his 66th and his 67th, depending on your year of birth). will be reduced accordingly. Alternatively, deferring benefits beyond full retirement age can result in higher monthly benefits. Consider factors such as financial need, life expectancy, and other sources of income after retirement when making this decision.

Maximizing social security benefits:

There are strategies for maximizing social security benefits. For example, if you are married, you are entitled to spousal benefits and may be entitled to a portion of your spouse's Social Security benefits. By understanding these strategies and working with your spouse, you can optimize your overall retirement income.

Retirement options and considerations:

If you receive your pension through your employer, you may need to make decisions about how you will receive your pension benefits. Common options include receiving a monthly annuity or paying a lump sum. Each option has advantages and disadvantages. Consider factors such as life expectancy, financial goals, risk tolerance, and the stability of your retirement savings when deciding between these options.

Evaluation of the annuity purchase offer:

In some cases, an employer may offer to purchase an annuity with a lump sum in exchange for waiving the right to future annuity payments. Evaluating these offers requires careful consideration. We assess factors such as your current financial situation, expected return on investment, and the reliability of your employer's financial situation. It may be beneficial to consult a financial advisor or pension planner to analyze the long-term impact of purchasing an annuity.

Integration of social security, pension and other retirement income:

Effective integration of social security benefits, pensions and all other sources of retirement income is essential. By strategically aligning these sources of income, you can optimize your overall retirement cash flow and ensure a stable and sustainable income in retirement.

Diploma:

Planning for retirement means making decisions about your Social Security benefits and your pension. Stay informed by understanding how Social Security benefits work, determining when benefits start, maximizing benefits, evaluating retirement options, and effectively integrating different income sources.

You can make decisions to meet your financial goals based on This chapter provides an overview of the decisions to be made regarding Social Security and pensions, providing opportunities to optimize your retirement income and achieve financial security during your golden years.Â

CHAPTER 7:

Insurance and risk management

Introduction:

Insurance plays an important role in our lives by providing protection and financial security against the unexpected. This chapter covers the basics of insurance and risk management. Understanding different types of insurance, assessing insurance needs, reviewing policies and coverages, and implementing effective insurance planning strategies are important steps in ensuring financial well-being. is.

Part 1:
Understand types of insurance (health insurance, life insurance, car insurance, home insurance)

Insurance is a contract between an individual and an insurance company that provides financial compensation in the event of certain risks or losses. To build a solid foundation in personal finance, it is important to understand the different types of insurance available to individuals. This section provides an overview of the most common types of insurance such as health insurance, life insurance, auto insurance, and home insurance. We consider the purpose, coverage and benefits of each type to help you make an informed decision when choosing the right coverage for your specific needs.

Section 2:
Assessment of insurance needs

Assessing insurance needs is an important step in effective risk management. This section describes the process of assessing insurance needs based on various factors such as age, dependents, lifestyle and financial burden. We delve into the importance of a comprehensive analysis of risk exposures to identify potential coverage gaps. By understanding your own situation, you can make informed decisions about the type and level of insurance that best suits your personal and financial goals.

Section 3:
Navigate policies and coverage

Insurance policies can be complex documents full of industry jargon and intricate details. This section describes the process of demystifying an insurance contract and understanding its components. Learn about the most important terms, conditions and exclusions often found in insurance contracts. It also explains the importance of reading and comparing policies, deductibles, premiums and limits. With this knowledge, you will be able to better navigate your insurance policy and gain a clear understanding of what coverage is offered and any limitations or exclusions that may exist.

Section 4:
Risk mitigation through proper insurance planning

Insurance planning is the process of strategically selecting and managing insurance policies to minimize financial risk. The final section of this chapter discusses effective insurance planning strategies to mitigate risk. It explains the concept of risk transfer and the role insurance companies play in transferring potential losses from individuals to insurance companies. We also consider risk management techniques such as policy bundling, deductible adjustments, and coverage limit assessments. Having a good insurance plan in place can ensure your financial health and protect your assets from the unexpected.

Diploma:

Insurance and risk management are an integral part of personal finances. Understand different types of insurance, assess insurance needs, manage policies and coverage, and implement effective insurance planning strategies to help you make informed decisions and achieve financial stability. You will be able to protect The next few chapters delve deeper into advanced insurance concepts and consider additional strategies for optimizing financial well-being.

Understand Types Of Insurance

Introduction:

Insurance is an important aspect of personal finances, providing protection and financial security against unforeseen events and risks. This chapter discusses different types of insurance, such as health insurance, life insurance, auto insurance, and home insurance. Understanding these types of insurance can help you make informed decisions about the insurance coverage you need to protect your financial well-being.

Part 1:
Health insurance

Health insurance is a type of insurance that covers medical expenses. It plays a key role in controlling health care costs, accessing quality care, and protecting against the significant financial burden of unforeseen illnesses and accidents. This section covers the basics of health insurance, including different insurance types, coverage options, and considerations when choosing health insurance. Understanding health insurance can help you make informed decisions about your health and financial needs.

Section 2:
Life insurance

A life insurance policy is a contract between an individual and an insurance company that provides financial protection to a beneficiary in the event of the policyholder's death. An essential tool for ensuring the financial security of your loved ones in the event of an untimely death. This section covers types of life insurance such as: B. It explains term and life insurance and helps you understand the factors to consider when choosing life insurance. Understanding life insurance can help you make decisions that meet your financial goals and meet your family's future financial needs.

Section 3:
auto insurance

Auto insurance is a type of insurance that compensates for economic losses due to vehicle accidents, theft, damage, etc. This is a legal requirement in many countries and aims to reduce the financial risks associated with owning and operating a vehicle. This section examines key elements of a car insurance policy, including third party liability, collision insurance, and collision damage waivers. We also discuss the factors that affect car insurance premiums and offer tips for choosing the right coverage for your specific needs.

Section 4:
household insurance

Homeowners insurance, also known as homeowners insurance, is designed to protect your property and belongings from a variety of hazards such as fire, theft, and natural disasters. Whether you own a home or rent an apartment, home contents insurance provides essential protection for your home and personal belongings. This section covers the basics of home insurance, including coverage, exclusions, and considerations when purchasing home insurance. Understanding home insurance can help protect your investment and reduce the financial risks associated with home ownership.

Diploma:

Understanding the different types of insurance, such as health insurance, life insurance, auto insurance, and home insurance, is critical to building a strong foundation in your personal finances. Understanding the basics of each type of insurance will help you make informed decisions about the coverage you need to protect yourself, your loved ones, and your assets. The next sections of this chapter look at assessing insurance needs, managing insurance policies and coverage, and mitigating risk with good insurance planning. All of these are essential to achieving financial stability and peace of mind.

Assessment Of Insurance Needs

Introduction:

Assessing your insurance needs is an important step in managing risk and protecting your financial health. This chapter describes the process of assessing insurance needs to ensure adequate coverage. By understanding your particular situation and assessing the potential risks, you can make an informed decision about the type and amount of insurance that best suits your needs.

Part 1:
Assessing your personal and financial situation

Assessing your insurance needs begins with assessing your personal and financial situation. This section reviews the main factors that can affect your insurance needs. Discuss aspects such as your age, marital status, family status, and general health. Additionally, review financial commitments such as outstanding debt, mortgages, and future financial goals. Considering these factors will give you a complete understanding of the risks you face and the insurance coverage you need to mitigate those risks.

Section 2:
identify potential risks

To accurately assess your insurance needs, it is important to understand the potential risks you may be exposed to. This section will help you identify specific risks that may affect your life, property and financial stability. We cover a wide range of risks, including health risks, accidents, natural disasters, and liability risks. Recognizing these potential threats can help you determine the appropriate insurance to protect you and your assets from financial loss.

Section 3:

Estimated need for compensation

Once you have identified the risks you face, the next step is to estimate the amount of coverage you need for each type of insurance. This section provides guidance for evaluating coverage for health insurance, life insurance, auto insurance, home insurance, and other related types of insurance. Discuss factors such as deductibles, insurance limits, and exclusions that may affect your insurance needs. Accurately assessing your coverage needs can help ensure you have adequate protection without overpaying for coverage you don't need.

Section 4:
Review of existing insurance coverage

If you already have an insurance policy, it is important to periodically review your existing insurance coverage to ensure that it meets your current needs. This section describes the process for reviewing policies and coverage. Learn about the importance of staying up to date on changes in your personal circumstances that may require adjustments to your policy terms, exclusions and coverage. Regularly reviewing your insurance coverage will help you maintain an adequate level of protection and avoid coverage gaps.

Diploma:

Assessing your insurance needs is an important step in effectively managing risk and safeguarding your financial stability. By assessing your personal and financial situation, identifying potential risks, assessing your insurance needs and reviewing your existing insurance coverage, you will be better informed about the policy that best meets your needs. You can make informed decisions. The next sections of this chapter describe how to manage policies and coverage, how to mitigate risk through good insurance planning, and provide practical guidance for optimizing insurance coverage while maximizing cost efficiency. provide strategy.

Navigate Policies And Coverage

Introduction:

To effectively manage risk and ensure adequate protection, it is important to review insurance policies and understand the terms of coverage. This chapter delves into the intricacies of an insurance contract and walks you through the process of understanding its constituent parts. Mastering the art of choosing the right policy and coverage can help you make informed decisions, optimize coverage, and protect your financial well-being.

Part 1:
Understand Terms of Use

Insurance policies can be complex documents filled with technical terms and conditions. In this section, we will clarify the language of the insurance contract and outline the terms and conditions of the various insurance contracts. Learn important terms such as premiums, deductibles, insurance limits, and disclaimers. Understanding these terms will enable you to read and interpret insurance policies effectively and provide a clear understanding of the insurance coverage and limitations provided.

Section 2:
Explore cover types and options

Insurance coverage varies greatly depending on the policy you choose and the type of insurance. This section reviews the different types of coverage and options available in various insurance policies. It describes the types of risks covered, the level of protection offered and the specific circumstances under which the indemnification applies. Understanding insurance types and options, such as health insurance, life insurance, auto insurance, and home insurance, can help you choose the policy that fits your needs and provides the right level of protection.

Section 3:
Evaluating Policy Provisions and Exclusions

Insurance terms and exclusions play an important role in determining the coverage provided by an insurance policy. This section details the policy terms and exclusions and what they mean. Learn about common exclusions included in insurance contracts and how they affect your coverage. It also supports the evaluation of insurance terms. B. Coverage, Waiting Periods, and Claim Resolution Procedures. Understanding these terms and exclusions will help you assess the suitability of your insurance policy and make an informed decision about the coverage you need.

Section 4:
Comparing insurance policies and insurance companies

To navigate insurance policies effectively, it is important to compare different insurance policies and insurance companies. This section provides strategies and tips for comparing insurance companies and providers. Learn about factors to consider, including premium rates, insurer financial health, customer service, claims processing, and more. A thorough comparison will help you choose insurance from reputable providers who offer competitive terms, reliable coverage and excellent customer support.

Diploma:

Familiarity with insurance policies and understanding of coverage terms are critical to safeguarding financial health and effectively managing risk. Understanding insurance terms, reviewing insurance types and options, evaluating policy terms and exclusions, and comparing policies and insurance companies helps you make informed decisions about coverage. increase. The next section of this chapter explores risk mitigation through good insurance planning and offers practical strategies for optimizing insurance coverage while maximizing cost efficiency.

Risk Mitigation Through Proper Insurance Planning

Introduction:

Risk mitigation is an important aspect of financial stability and a good insurance plan is an important tool for managing and minimizing potential risks. This chapter reviews insurance risk management concepts and shows how to develop a comprehensive insurance plan. By understanding the importance of mitigating risk and implementing effective insurance strategies, you will be better equipped to protect yourself, your loved ones and your assets from financial hardship.

Part 1:
Identify and prioritize risks

To effectively mitigate risk through insurance planning, it is important to identify and prioritize the potential risks you face. This section will help you assess the risks associated with your personal and financial situation. Discusses common risks such as accident, illness, disability, property damage, and liability. By understanding the specific risks associated with your situation, you can prioritize insurance coverage that offers the highest level of protection and security.

Section 2:
Choosing the Right Coverage

Once you have identified the risks that need to be mitigated, the next step is choosing the right insurance. This section will guide you through the process of evaluating and selecting the appropriate insurance policy and coverage options. Learn the factors to consider when determining the appropriate coverage level. B. Asset Value, Potential Risk of Loss, and Financial Obligations. Choosing the right hedging can provide adequate protection against potential risks.

Section 3:
Insurance plan review and renewal

Insurance planning is an ongoing process that requires regular review and updating. This section emphasizes the importance of regularly reviewing your insurance plan to ensure it meets your changing needs. We will consult with you about life events that require adjustment of coverage, such as marriage, childbirth, and changing jobs. By being proactive and keeping your insurance plan up to date, you can maintain optimal coverage and avoid potential coverage gaps.

Section 4:
Optimization of insurance costs

Insurance is essential for managing risk, but optimizing insurance costs is also important. This section offers practical strategies for reducing your premiums without sacrificing the coverage you need. Consider options such as bundling policies, increasing deductibles, and considering discounts and loyalty programs. By optimizing insurance costs, you can balance affordability and comprehensive coverage to maximize the value of your insurance investment.

<u>Diploma:</u>

<u>Risk mitigation through proper insurance planning is an important aspect of personal finances and financial stability. By identifying and prioritizing risks, selecting appropriate insurance coverage, reviewing and updating insurance plans, and optimizing insurance costs, you can effectively protect yourself and your financial well-being. increase.</u>

CHAPTER 8:

Building a strong credit score

Part 1:
Importance of good credit

Good credit is a fundamental aspect of personal finance and affects many areas of financial life. It acts as a measure of your creditworthiness, affecting your ability to secure credit, earn favorable interest rates, and even your eligibility for certain jobs and housing. In this section, we explore why good credit is important and how it positively impacts financial well-being.

Section 2:
Factors Affecting Creditworthiness

Understanding the factors that affect your credit score is critical to effective management and improvement. This section describes the key factors that contribute to your credit score, including: B. Payment History, Credit Usage, Credit History Length, Credit Mix, and New Credit Requests. Understanding these factors can help you identify areas where you can make positive changes to improve your credit score.

Section 3:
Build and maintain a healthy credit score

Building a healthy credit score requires a combination of responsible financial behavior and patience. This section covers the steps necessary to build a strong credit history, including opening credit accounts, making payments on time, and maintaining a low credit utilization rate. It also explains the importance of regularly monitoring your credit report, promptly correcting any errors or discrepancies, and using credit responsibly to maintain a long credit history.

Section 4:
Strategies for improving a low credit score

If your current credit score is low, don't worry. There are effective strategies for improving your credit score. This section provides practical tips and techniques that can help improve your credit score in the long run. Consider methods such as creating a repayment plan, prioritizing debt repayment, negotiating with creditors, and using credit-building tools such as secured credit cards and credit-building loans. By implementing these strategies, you can gradually rebuild your creditworthiness and increase your financial opportunities.

Diploma

This chapter has shown the importance of building a good credit score and provided insight into the factors that influence it. We discussed the steps to establish and maintain a healthy credit score and suggested strategies to improve low credit scores. By applying the knowledge and implementing the strategies outlined in this chapter, you will be able to master your credit score and pave the way to a more secure financial future. Remember that building good reputation is a long-term commitment that requires discipline and responsible financial management, but it is well worth the effort.

Importance Of Good Credit

Your credit score plays an important role in your financial life.

This is a numerical representation of your creditworthiness and provides lenders, landlords and other financial institutions with an assessment of your ability to manage debt responsibly. Good credit is essential for many reasons, but this section explores its importance in more detail.

1.1 Loan and Credit Eligibility

When you apply for a loan or credit card, lenders evaluate your creditworthiness based on your credit history. A good credit score increases your chances of getting a loan, mortgage, or credit card approved. You can also take advantage of higher credit limits and lower interest rates, saving you money in the long run.

1.2 Falling interest rates

A good credit rating indicates that you are a low-risk borrower, which means lower interest rates on loans and credit cards. With credit, you can take out a loan at a lower interest rate, save money on interest payments, and potentially pay off your debt faster.

1.3 Rent a house

Landlords often assess the creditworthiness of potential tenants to determine their reliability and financial responsibility. A good credit rating increases your chances of securing a coveted rental property and negotiating favorable rental terms. This gives landlords confidence that they will pay their rent on time and meet their financial obligations throughout the tenancy.

1.4 Employment Opportunities

In some industries, employers may check your creditworthiness as part of the hiring process. Good credit can prove your financial responsibility and credibility, and may improve your prospects when applying for jobs that involve financial responsibility or require security clearance.

1.5 Utility and Service Providers

Your provider may consider your creditworthiness when setting up public services or signing up for a cell phone plan. A good credit rating may give you more favorable terms, such as a lower down payment or no set-up fees, when using these important services.

1.6 Access to economic opportunities

Good credit opens the door to many financial opportunities, such as obtaining lower premiums, securing business financing, and participating in exclusive credit card reward programs. This gives you more options and flexibility to effectively manage your finances.

Diploma

Understanding the importance of good credit is the first step to building a strong financial foundation. It opens up a world of financial opportunities, from securing credit at low interest rates to accessing better rental options and employment opportunities. In the next few sections, we'll look at the factors that affect your credit score, strategies for building and maintaining a healthy credit score, and techniques for improving a bad credit score. By applying the knowledge and implementing the strategies outlined in this chapter, you can take control of your credit score and start on your path to financial success.

Factors Affecting Creditworthiness

Your credit score is influenced by several factors that assess your creditworthiness and financial responsibility. Understanding these factors is essential to effectively managing your credit score and improving your credit rating over the long term. In this section, we look at the main factors that affect your credit score.

2.1 Payment history

Your payment history is one of the most important factors that affect your credit score. This reflects whether you are paying your debts on time and whether you have a history of late payments or defaults. Consistently making payments on time demonstrates your credibility and commitment as a borrower and has a positive effect on your creditworthiness.

2.2 Use of Credits

Credit usage refers to the amount of available credits that you are currently using. This is calculated by dividing the outstanding credit card balance by the total credit limit. Keeping the loan utilization rate low, ideally below his 30%, shows the lender that he is responsible for his loans and not overly dependent on borrowed funds. Low credit utilization can have a positive impact on your credit score.

2.3 Credit history length

The length of your credit history plays a role in determining your creditworthiness. Lenders prefer borrowers with longer credit histories as they allow for a more comprehensive record of their financial behavior. If you have a short credit history, it can be difficult to build good credit quickly. However, maintaining a good payment history over the long term will help build a solid foundation for your credit score.

2.4 Credit mix

Credit mix refers to the different types of credit accounts you have, such as credit cards, loans, and mortgages. Having different credit accounts shows that you can manage different types of credit responsibly. However, it is important to note that opening multiple credit accounts just to diversify your credit mix can have negative consequences if not properly managed.

2.5 New Credit Request

Every time you apply for new credit, such as a credit card or a loan, the demands are added to your credit report. Too many demanding demands in a short period of time can worry lenders and affect your credit score. We recommend that you limit the number of loan applications and apply for a loan only when you need it.

Diploma

Understanding the factors that affect your credit score can give you valuable insight into how to effectively manage your credit score. Manage your credit score and improve your financial performance by maintaining a good payment history, keeping credit utilization low, building a longer credit history, responsibly diversifying your credit mix, and minimizing new credit requests. can be improved. In the next few sections, we'll look at strategies for building and maintaining a healthy credit score, as well as techniques for improving a bad credit score. By applying the knowledge outlined in this chapter and implementing the strategies, you will have the tools to build a strong credit profile and achieve financial success.

Build And Maintain A Healthy Credit Score

Building and maintaining a good credit rating is an ongoing

process that requires responsible financial practices and strategic planning. This section will guide you through the steps you need to take to build a strong credit history and ensure a long-lasting good credit rating.

3.1 Open a credit account

To start building your credit score, consider opening a credit account, such as a credit card or a small personal loan. A valid credit account proves your ability to manage your debt responsibly. However, it is important to use your credit wisely and not take on more debt than you can comfortably handle.

3.2 Make Timely Payments

Consistently making payments on time is important to maintaining a healthy credit score. Late payments can negatively affect your credit score. Therefore, it is important to pay your bills on time. Don't forget to pay by setting reminders and automatic payments. It is important to pay at least the minimum amount on your credit card, but even better to pay the full balance if possible.

3.3 Keep your credit usage low

Credit Usage refers to the amount of credit you are currently using relative to your total credit limit and is an important factor in determining your creditworthiness. Try to keep your credit usage below 30%. For example, if you have a credit card with a limit of $1,000, try to keep your outstanding balance under $300. Keeping your credit utilization low shows the lender that you're not overly dependent on borrowed funds.

3.4 Maintain a long credit history

The length of your credit history is an important part of your credit score. Building a solid credit history takes time, so having the oldest credit account is an advantage. Older credit cards have a longer credit history, so don't block them unless absolutely necessary. Older accounts with good payment history can have a positive impact on your credit score.

3.5 Monitor your credit report

Regularly monitoring your credit report helps you keep your credit activities up to date and spot any errors or discrepancies that can affect your credit score. You are entitled to receive a free copy of your credit report from the major credit bureaus (Equifax, Experian, TransUnion) once a year. Check your credit report for errors and contact the credit bureaus to correct any errors immediately.

3.6 Use Credits Responsibly

Responsible credit management is essential to building and maintaining a healthy credit score. Avoid using up your credit card limit and only take on debt that you can comfortably manage. Be mindful of your spending habits and create a budget that prioritizes paying off debt and using credit responsibly. Demonstrating responsible lending behavior creates a positive credit profile.

Diploma

Building and maintaining good credit is an important aspect of personal finances. By following the steps outlined in this chapter (opening credit accounts, making payments on time, maintaining low credit utilization, maintaining a long credit history, monitoring your credit report, and using credit responsibly), you can build strong credit. You can establish a foundation. . Remember that building good reputation is a long-term commitment that requires discipline and responsible financial management. However, with dedicated effort and informed decision-making, it is possible to achieve a healthy credit score, which opens up many financial opportunities and contributes to overall financial stability.

Strategies For Improving A Low Credit Score

If your current credit score is low, don't worry. There are effective strategies for improving your credit score. This section provides practical tips and techniques to improve your credit score over time and restore your financial stability.

4.1 Create a repayment plan
Start creating a repayment plan to deal with outstanding debts and late payments. Prioritize paying off high-interest debt first, as reducing your debt burden can have a positive impact on your credit score. Set a budget to spend a portion of your monthly income on debt repayments and stick to it.

4.2 Pay on time
To improve your credit score, it's important to consistently make payments on time. Set payment reminders and automatic payments to never miss a deadline. Paying your bills on time will help you demonstrate financial responsibility and restore trust from your lenders.

4.3 Negotiations with creditors
If you have difficulty meeting your financial obligations, you should contact your creditors. Explain your situation and consider the possibility of negotiating new repayment terms, such as lower interest rates or expanded payment plans. Many creditors are willing to work with you to find a mutually beneficial solution.

4.4 Pay off debt
Reducing your overall debt is a key strategy for improving your

credit score. Make sure you pay at least the minimum amount on your credit card each month. Paying off debt reduces your use of credit, which can have a positive impact on your credit score.

4.5 Use credit building tools
If you're struggling to get traditional credit due to a bad credit score, consider using a credit building tool. A secure credit card or credit building loan can help you build a good payment history and restore your creditworthiness. These tools require a down payment or security deposit. This minimizes lender risk and allows you to demonstrate responsible credit usage.

4.6 Monitor your credit report
Regularly monitoring your credit report is essential to track progress and ensure accuracy. Look for errors. B. False personal information or accounts that do not belong to you. Please report any inaccuracies to the credit bureaus and follow up to ensure they are corrected immediately.

4.7 Patience and Patience
Improving a low credit score takes time and patience. It is important that we continue to persevere and advocate for responsible economic practices. Building good credit is a gradual process, but consistent, positive behavior can help build trust over time.

Diploma

Improving a low credit score is an achievable goal with the right strategy and determination. Gradually build credit by developing a repayment plan, making payments on time, negotiating with creditors, paying off debt, using credit building tools, monitoring your credit report, and exercising patience and perseverance. Improve your score and take back control of your financial situation. future. Remember that building a good credit score takes discipline and dedication, but it's well worth the effort. With consistent effort over time, you can achieve financial stability and open the door to better financial opportunities.

CHAPTER 9:

Wealth Accumulation and Financial Independence

Here we delve deeper into the basic concepts of wealth building and financial independence. Understanding these principles is critical to laying a solid foundation on your path to financial success. By the end of this chapter, you will have a solid understanding of the key strategies and principles that will help you reach your financial goals.

Part 1:
Understanding the Principles of Wealth Creation

Accumulation of wealth is not the result of luck or chance. This is a conscious process that requires knowledge, discipline, and consistent effort. This section reviews the basic principles of wealth building and lays the foundation for your financial journey. Learn the importance of setting clear financial goals, controlling spending, and developing a wealth-creation-focused mindset.

Section 2:
Generate multiple revenue streams

One of the keys to building wealth is diversifying your income streams. Relying solely on a single salary can expose you to unforeseen financial problems. This section explores different strategies for generating multiple revenue streams.

From exploring side hustle to starting a business to investing in income-generating assets, you'll discover the power to create additional streams of income and how it can accelerate your path to financial independence.

Section 3:
Strategies for long-term wealth building

Building wealth is a marathon, not a sprint. It requires a long-term approach and strategic planning. This section discusses effective strategies for long-term wealth accumulation. Learn about the power of compound interest, the benefits of investing in assets such as stocks, bonds and real estate, and the importance of developing a well-diversified investment portfolio. It also covers the concept of risk management and how to make informed decisions to protect and grow your wealth over the long term.

Section 4:
On the Road to Financial Independence

Financial independence is the ultimate goal for many people to take control of their financial life. It refers to a state in which people can freely pursue their desired lifestyle without relying on conventional employment by covering their living expenses with unearned income from investments, etc. This section describes the steps and strategies you can take to work towards financial independence. Explore concepts such as the 4% rule, retirement savings and investments, and creating a sustainable financial plan that fits your goals and aspirations.

By the end of this chapter, you will have a solid understanding of the principles and strategies necessary to build wealth and achieve financial independence. Remember that building wealth is a journey that requires dedication, perseverance and continued education. Take this transformative path to mastering your money and controlling your financial future.

Understanding The Principles Of Wealth Creation

This section examines the basic principles underlying the wealth creation process. Understanding these principles is critical as it provides a framework for building a strong financial foundation and achieving long-term financial independence.

Principle 1:
Mindset and goal setting

Wealth building starts with having the right mindset. A positive and positive attitude towards money and financial success is essential. First, set clear financial goals that align with your aspirations and values. Define both short-term and long-term goals that serve as milestones on your wealth journey. A clear vision and goals help you stay focused and motivated.

Principle 2:
budget and save

Budgeting is the foundation of financial management. It's all about monitoring your income and expenses to make sure you're living within your means. Creating a budget helps you prioritize spending, identify areas for cuts, and allocate funds for savings and investments. Regularly saving a portion of your income is very important for wealth accumulation as it provides the necessary funds to create future wealth.

Principle 3:
debt management

Effective debt management is another important aspect of wealth building. Prioritize paying off high-interest debt and develop a debt repayment plan. Avoid unnecessary debt and handle credit responsibly. Reducing the debt burden frees up resources for saving and investment, accelerating the wealth-building process.

Principle 4:
Investment and asset allocation

Investing is a powerful tool for building wealth. Learn about different investment options such as stocks, bonds, real estate and mutual funds. Understand the concept of risk and return and diversify your investments to minimize risk. Asset allocation, or diversification of investments across different asset classes, is key to building a balanced and resilient investment portfolio.

Principle 5:
Compound interest and long-term growth

Harnessing the power of compound interest is essential for long-term wealth accumulation. By reinvesting your investment income, you not only earn interest on your principal, but also interest that accrues over time. The longer the investment period, the more likely it is that compound interest will work in your favor. By starting early and staying invested for the long term, you can significantly increase your wealth creation potential.

Principle 6:
Continuous learning and adaptation

Financial markets and economic conditions are constantly evolving. To build sustainable wealth, commit to lifelong learning. Stay up to date on financial trends, investment strategies and new opportunities. Be open to adjusting your financial plans as circumstances change. By staying informed and adaptable, you can make informed decisions and take advantage of wealth-building opportunities.

Understanding and applying these wealth-building principles will lay a solid foundation for your financial journey. Subsequent sections of this chapter, and throughout the book, provide practical examples of how to apply these principles effectively, generate multiple streams of income, accumulate wealth over time, and ultimately achieve financial independence. Consider your strategy. Remember that accumulating wealth is a process that requires dedication, perseverance, and discipline. However, with the right knowledge and tools, you can take control of your financial future and work towards achieving your financial goals.

Strategies For Long-Term Wealth Building

This section examines effective strategies for long-term wealth accumulation. These strategies enable us to make informed decisions, optimize our financial resources, and work towards lasting financial stability and independence.

Set clear financial goals.

Before embarking on your wealth building journey, it is important to define your financial goals. Identify what you want to achieve in the long term. B. Saving for retirement, buying a home, or paying for a child's education. Setting specific, measurable, achievable, relevant, and time-bound (SMART) goals gives you a clear roadmap and keeps you focused. Create a comprehensive financial plan.

Careful financial planning is essential for long-term wealth accumulation. It should include budgeting, savings, investments and effective debt management. Set a realistic budget that fits your goals and priorities, and use some of your income to save and invest. A financial plan serves as a guide to help you make informed financial decisions and ensure that your goals are met.

Invest for the long term:

Investing is an important strategy for building wealth. Start early and take advantage of compound interest. Consider investing in a diversified portfolio that fits your risk tolerance and investment goals. Long-term investment vehicles such as retirement accounts, index funds, and exchange-traded funds (ETFs) can help you capture market potential while managing risk.

Maintain disciplined savings habits:
Continual savings are essential for long-term wealth accumulation. Automate your savings by setting up automatic transfers from your income to another savings or investment account. Treat savings as regular spending and prioritize it over discretionary spending. Try to keep saving some of your income, even during times of economic abundance.

Minimize your debt and manage your credit wisely.
Debt can hinder your efforts to build wealth. Make a plan to pay off high-interest debt as soon as possible. Prioritize high-interest debt first while paying all debts in a timely manner. Borrow responsibly, borrow only when you need to, and pay when it's convenient for you.

Diversify your wealth:
Diversification is an important risk management strategy in wealth building. Spread your investments across different asset classes such as stocks, bonds, real estate and commodities. Diversification reduces the impact of market volatility and reduces the risks associated with relying on a single investment.

Educate yourself continuously:
Get the latest information on financial trends, investment strategies and growth opportunities. Expand your knowledge by reading books, attending seminars, listening to podcasts, and following renowned financial experts. Continuing education

enables you to make informed financial decisions and adapt to changing market conditions.

Remember that long-term wealth accumulation is a step-by-step process that requires patience, discipline, and perseverance. It's important to review your strategy regularly and adjust it as necessary to ensure it's aligned with your changing financial circumstances and goals.

Incorporating these strategies into your financial planning can increase your wealth potential, improve your financial prospects, and bring you closer to the financial independence you desire.

Be proactive, stay focused, and take the necessary steps to lay a solid foundation for long-term wealth building. With the right strategy and a positive mindset, you can start on your path to financial success and enjoy the freedom and security that comes with achieving your financial goals.

Generate Multiple Revenue Streams

This section explores the concept of generating multiple streams of income as a powerful strategy for improving financial security, accelerating wealth accumulation, and achieving economic independence.

Sources of income refer to sources that generate money. Relying on a single source of income, such as a paycheck from a job, can limit economic growth and leave people vulnerable to unforeseen changes. Diversifying your income streams can reduce risk, increase your earning potential, and create opportunities for long-term wealth accumulation.

Here are some key strategies for generating multiple revenue streams.

Side hustle and freelance work:
Consider using your skills, talents, and hobbies to start a side business or offer freelance services. It can be anything from graphic design to writing to consulting to tutoring to selling products online. A side hustle generates additional income and provides valuable growth and exploration opportunities.

Unearned Income:
Passive sources of income allow you to make money with minimal ongoing effort. This may include rental properties, dividends from investments, royalties for intellectual property, and the creation and sale of digital products. Building a passive income stream can provide a steady flow of cash and contribute to long-term wealth accumulation.

Investment return:
Investing in stocks, bonds, mutual funds, real estate, and other investment vehicles generates income through capital appreciation, dividends, or interest payments. By carefully choosing investments and diversifying your portfolio, you can establish a reliable source of income and benefit from long-term market growth.

Rental income:
Owning or renting property, whether residential or commercial, provides a steady stream of income. Your real estate investment will appreciate in value over time, while also providing rental income to cover your expenses and help you reach your overall financial goals.

Online business and e-commerce:
The digital world presents huge opportunities to generate revenue

streams through online and e-commerce businesses. Sell your products and services online, join affiliate marketing programs, and develop and monetize popular websites and blogs.

Creating multiple revenue streams not only increases your earning potential, but also gives you greater security and flexibility in your financial situation. Diversification helps us weather economic downturns and job market volatility, and provides a buffer against unexpected economic setbacks.

However, it's important to note that building multiple revenue streams takes effort, time, and dedication. You can balance work and side hustle, continuous learning, and adapting to new opportunities. In addition, careful financial planning and budgeting are essential to effectively manage revenues generated from various sources.

By incorporating these strategies into your financial planning, you can strengthen your financial position, accelerate wealth accumulation, and ultimately work towards achieving financial independence.

Remember, building multiple revenue streams is a dynamic process that requires constant effort and adaptability. With determination and the right attitude, you can create new income opportunities, take control of your financial future, and pave the way to a richer, more fulfilling life.

On The Road To Financial Independence

This section explores the concept of financial independence and offers strategies to help you work towards achieving this important milestone. Financial independence refers to a state in which income from a variety of sources is sufficient to support one's living expenses and desired lifestyle without dependence on conventional or active work.

Define your vision of financial independence.
First, imagine what financial independence means for you personally. Think about the lifestyle you want, the level of financial security you want to achieve, and the activities you want to do without financial constraints. Defining your vision of financial independence gives you a clear goal to work towards and the motivation you need to keep trying. Calculate your financial independence.
To determine how much wealth you need to achieve financial independence, calculate your Financial Independence Score. This is the amount you will need annually to cover your living expenses. Start tracking your current spending and analyze your spending behavior. Consider factors such as housing, transportation, nutrition, health care, and discretionary spending. Calculate your financial independence score by multiplying your annual spending by the number of years you expect to be financially independent. Increase your savings rate:
One of the most important keys to achieving financial independence is increasing the savings rate. Save a good chunk of your income by thinking frugally and prioritizing savings over overspending. Review your budget, reduce spending, and identify areas where you can allocate more funds to saving and investing. The higher your savings rate, the faster you can build the wealth you need to become financially independent.

Invest to generate income:
Building a portfolio of income-generating assets is critical to achieving financial independence. Invest in dividend-paying stocks, bonds, rental properties, or other investments that generate regular income. Focus on creating a diversified investment portfolio that meets your risk tolerance and financial objectives. The return you earn from your investment will help

support you while you are financially independent.

Develop passive income streams.

Passive sources of income can greatly contribute to your journey to financial independence. Look for ways to generate passive income. B. Developing and selling digital products, affiliate marketing, or owning and renting real estate. Passive income provides steady cash flow without the need for ongoing active participation, giving you more freedom and flexibility.

Continuously monitor and adjust your plan.

Financial independence is a long-term goal that requires regular monitoring and adjustment of financial plans. Keep track of your progress towards financial independence and reassess your investments and income streams regularly. Be prepared to make changes if necessary to ensure your desired level of financial independence is on track.

Remember that the path to financial independence requires discipline, perseverance, and perseverance. Building the wealth and income streams you need may take time, but every step you take brings you closer to your goals.

By implementing these strategies and adhering to your financial goals, you can take control of your financial future and create a life of freedom and prosperity.

Financial independence is within reach. With commitment and the right strategy, you can break free from financial constraints and create the life you've always dreamed of. Together, let's embark on this exciting journey and work toward achieving the

financial independence you deserve.

CHAPTER 10:

Money Psychology

Money doesn't just mean numbers and transactions. It is closely related to our emotions, prejudices and ways of thinking. Understanding the psychology of money is an important first step to mastering finance. This chapter examines different aspects of our relationship with money and how it affects our financial decisions. By recognizing and addressing these psychological factors, you can develop healthier habits, overcome challenges, and lay a solid foundation for financial success.

Emotions and biases in financial decision making
Money has the power to evoke strong emotions within us. Whether it's the joy of financial good fortune or the fear of mounting debt, our emotions play a large role in shaping our financial decisions. Additionally, we tend to have cognitive biases that can cloud our judgment and lead to irrational financial decisions.

This section looks at common sentiments and biases that influence financial decisions. We explore the impact of fear, greed and social comparison on our spending habits, investment decisions and overall financial well-being. By understanding these emotional and cognitive biases, we can learn how to recognize and mitigate their impact so we can make more rational and informed financial decisions. Addressing common challenges in how we think about money
Our thoughts and beliefs about money are shaped by many factors, including our upbringings, social influences, and personal

experiences. These beliefs can empower us to be financially successful or prevent us from realizing our true potential.

This part of the chapter covers some of the most common money thinking challenges and explores techniques for overcoming them. We will explore scarcity and abundance mindsets, the impact of self-limiting beliefs, and the importance of cultivating a growth mindset for money. By challenging and redefining our limiting beliefs, we can unlock new possibilities and build positive and empowering relationships with money. Develop healthy money habits and attitudes

Building a strong financial foundation takes more than knowledge. It requires developing healthy habits and attitudes towards money. This section will focus on practical strategies for developing positive money habits and attitudes that align with your financial goals.

We will explore the concept of financial health and its components such as budgeting, saving and investing. We discuss the importance of setting clear financial goals, creating budgets that reflect our values, and implementing strategies for wise saving and investing. Additionally, it emphasizes the importance of financial self-care and the role of mindfulness in managing your financial life. By developing healthy money habits and maintaining a positive attitude towards money, we can transform our economic activity into a fulfilling, purposeful and sustainable one.

Diploma

Understanding the psychology of money is an important foundation for mastering personal finance. By examining the emotions and prejudices that influence our financial decisions, overcoming common money attitude challenges, and developing healthy money habits and attitudes, we can improve our financial You can control your life.

Emotions And Biases In Financial Decision Making

Our relationship with money goes beyond numbers and transactions. It is strongly influenced by our emotions and prejudices. This chapter explores the fascinating world of money psychology and how our emotions and biases influence our financial decisions. Understanding these psychological factors is critical to managing finances and making informed decisions. In this section, we look at emotions and biases that play an important role in shaping financial decisions.

The role of emotion in financial decision making
Money has a huge impact on our emotions. It can evoke feelings of joy, security and freedom, but it can also cause stress, anxiety and fear. These emotions can greatly influence the decisions we make regarding finances. For example, fear may lead us to avoid taking calculated risks or making investments that may prove profitable in the long run. On the other hand, the thrill of instant gratification can drive you to spend money impulsively, ignoring your long-term financial goals.

Understanding the emotional aspects of financial decision-making can help you develop strategies to effectively manage your emotions. We explore techniques for recognizing and treating emotional triggers, such as mindfulness practices and journaling, that can help you make more rational and balanced financial decisions.

Cognitive biases and their effects
Our minds are prone to various cognitive biases that can skew our judgment and lead to irrational financial decisions. These biases are automatic and unconscious thought patterns that can cloud our objectivity and prevent us from making informed decisions. Recognizing and understanding these biases is critical to overcoming their negative effects.

Consider common cognitive biases that influence financial decisions, such as:

a)   Loss avoidance:
Because we tend to fear losses more than we value gains, we can be overly risk averse and undermine our investment potential.

b) Confirmation error:
Our tendency to seek out information to support existing beliefs often leads to narrow vision and missed opportunities.

c) Anchor Bias:
We tend to rely too much on initial information when making decisions, which can prevent us from considering alternative options.

d) Herd mentality:
Our tendency to follow the crowd even when it's not to our advantage leads to crowd-oriented investment decisions.

Recognizing these biases can help us develop a more rational approach to financial decision making. Explore practical techniques such as conscious thinking, seeking different perspectives, and conducting thorough research to reduce the impact of bias on financial decisions.

Emotions and biases greatly influence our financial decisions. Understanding the role of emotions in shaping our relationship with money and recognizing the cognitive biases that can skew our judgments puts us in control of our financial lives. The next section of this chapter describes how to overcome common money mindset challenges that can help you develop a healthier and stronger view of money.

Addressing Common Challenges In How We Think About Money

The way we think plays an important role in our financial well-being. The way we think and feel about money can either lead to financial success or create obstacles to our progress. This chapter reviews common money-mind challenges that many face and offers strategies for overcoming them. By addressing these challenges head-on, we can build a healthy and powerful relationship with money.

Deficiency mentality vs. concept of abundance

One of the biggest challenges in how we think about money is how we think about scarcity. This mindset is rooted in the idea that wealth and resources are finite, leading to the fear of not having enough. It can manifest as hoarding, fear of spending, and reluctance to invest.

To overcome the scarcity mindset, we must cultivate the abundance mindset. This mindset is based on the belief that there is an abundance of opportunity, wealth and resources at your disposal. This includes shifting focus from scarcity to abundance, adopting a positive attitude, and recognizing the potential for growth and prosperity. We explore practical techniques such as gratitude exercises and visualization exercises to redefine our way of thinking and embrace abundance.

Self-Limiting Beliefs and Money Blocks

Self-limiting beliefs are deep-seated thoughts and beliefs that prevent us from achieving our financial goals. They often stem from our upbringing, social influences, or past experiences. Common self-limiting beliefs include, "Money is evil," "I am not worthy of wealth," or "I will never be financially successful."

Overcoming self-limiting beliefs requires self-awareness and a willingness to question and reframe them. Identifying these beliefs and discussing strategies for addressing them include: B. Seek affirmations, positive self-talk, and support from mentors and coaches. By replacing self-limiting beliefs with empowering beliefs, you can develop a mindset that supports your financial growth and success.

Develop a growth mindset for money

A growth mindset is the belief that our skills and intelligence can be developed through dedication, hard work and learning. Applying the growth mindset to finance allows us to view financial setbacks as opportunities for learning and growth. It encourages us to take calculated risks, seek out new knowledge, and persevere in the face of adversity. This section explores strategies for developing a growth mindset about money. Discuss the importance of lifelong learning, setting realistic goals, and accepting failure as a stepping stone to success. By adopting a growth mindset, you can transform your relationship with money from fear and stagnation to trust and continuous improvement.

Diploma

To master money management, it's important to overcome common challenges associated with money thinking. By moving from a scarcity mindset to an abundance mindset, challenging self-limiting beliefs, and cultivating a growth mindset for money, we can transform our financial lives. The next part of this chapter will cover developing healthy money habits and attitudes that will further strengthen your personal financial base.

Develop Healthy Money Habits And Attitudes

Our habits and attitudes towards money have a huge impact on our financial well-being. Developing healthy habits and maintaining a positive attitude can set you on the path to financial security and success. This chapter explores practical strategies for developing healthy money habits and promoting a positive attitude towards money.

Set clear financial goals
Setting clear financial goals is the foundation for building a strong financial future. This section describes the process of defining short-term and long-term financial goals. Discuss the importance of setting specific, measurable, achievable, relevant, and time-bound (SMART) goals. By clarifying your financial goals, you can create a roadmap for your financial efforts.

Create a budget that reflects your values
Budgeting is a basic tool for managing your money effectively. Get a clear picture of your finances by tracking your income, expenses and savings. This part of the chapter will guide you through creating a budget that aligns with your values â€‹â€‹and priorities. Here's a 50/30/20 household rule that suggests allocating 50% of your income to needs, 30% to wants, and 20% to savings and investments. It also provides tips on how to track your spending, cut unnecessary spending, and adjust your budget as circumstances change.

Save and invest wisely

Saving and investing are essential to long-term financial success. This section discusses the importance of saving for emergencies, future expenses, and retirement. We explore strategies for automating savings, setting up emergency funds, and maximizing savings growth through high-yield savings accounts and other investment vehicles. In addition, we will introduce you to the basics of investing, such as the different investment options available, risk management, and compounding opportunities. We emphasize the importance of diversifying your investments and seeking professional advice when necessary. By developing disciplined savings and investment habits, you can build wealth and reach your financial goals.

Practice financial self-care and mindfulness
Our interest in financial well-being goes beyond numbers and spreadsheets. It's about maintaining healthy relationships with money and practicing mindfulness.

Techniques such as meditation, journaling, and asking for support from loved ones can help create a sense of financial well-being and reduce financial anxiety.

Diploma

Developing healthy habits and healthy attitudes towards money is essential to mastering money management. By setting clear financial goals, creating a budget that reflects your values, saving and investing wisely, and practicing financial self-care and mindfulness, you can take control of your financial life. Combining the knowledge gained in this chapter with practical strategies will leave you well-prepared to make informed decisions and achieve lasting financial stability and success.

CHAPTER 11:

YOU DID IT

Congratulation! You've reached the end of Money Mastery 101.
A Comprehensive Guide to Personal Finance This book covers a wide range of topics to give you the knowledge and strategies you need to take control of your financial life. Implementing the principles and practices outlined in each chapter will achieve that and put you on the path to achieving financial stability and creating a prosperous future.

In this final chapter, let's review the key lessons we've covered so far and summarize the key points to remember.

Personal finances come first.
We started by understanding the importance of personal finance and how it affects our lives. By recognizing its importance and prioritizing it, you have already taken a big step towards financial success.

Set clear financial goals.
Setting clear and achievable financial goals is essential. These goals serve as landmarks and help you stay focused and motivated throughout your financial endeavors. Remember to make your goals specific, measurable, achievable, relevant and time bound (SMART).

Cultivate a positive attitude.

Developing a positive attitude towards money is very important. By changing our beliefs and attitudes, we can overcome challenges, seize opportunities, and make smart financial decisions. Believe in your ability to be financially successful. Then success will surely come. Build a strong financial base.

Budgeting forms the basis of your financial base. You can manage your finances by understanding your income, expenses, cash flow, and creating a personal budget. Effectively track and manage your spending and practice helpful savings tips to accelerate your progress.

Prioritize savings and emergency funds.
Saving money is essential for future financial stability. Separate short-term and long-term savings goals and build an emergency fund for unexpected expenses. Automate your savings to make the process easier and more consistent.

Debt management and reduction:
Debt can seriously damage your financial health. Understand different types of debt, implement strategies to manage and reduce it, and consider debt consolidation and refinancing options. With a clear plan, you can break free from debt and experience true financial freedom.

Accept investment principles.
Investing is a powerful tool for building wealth. Learn about different investment vehicles, assess your risk tolerance, and diversify your portfolio. Follow a long-term investment strategy and watch your assets grow over time.

Retirement plan:
Your golden years should be stress-free and financially stable. Understand the importance of retirement planning and explore different retirement accounts to maximize your savings. Make informed social security and pension decisions to optimize your retirement income. Protect yourself with insurance:
Risk mitigation is critical to financial stability. Assess your

insurance needs and understand different types of insurance. Find out about policies and insurance coverage to ensure you and your loved ones are protected should the unexpected occur.

Build and maintain a healthy credit score.
A good credit score opens the door to lucrative financial opportunities. Learn about the factors that affect your credit score and develop strategies for building and maintaining your credit score. Improve your bad credit by developing smart financial habits and addressing the underlying issues.

Wealth accumulation and financial independence goals:
Expand your thinking beyond just financial security. Discover wealth building principles, create multiple revenue streams, and adopt long-term wealth building strategies. Strive for financial independence. You are free to pursue your dreams without financial constraints.

Understand the psychology of money:
Recognize the role of emotions and biases in economic decision making. Overcome common money challenges and develop healthy money habits and attitudes. Understanding your relationship with money can help you make informed financial decisions.Â

Remember that mastering personal finance is a lifelong journey. Commit to continuous learning, adapt to changing financial conditions, and seek advice when needed. Adopt the principles and strategies outlined in this book and see how your financial situation changes.

In Money Mastery 101:
The Comprehensive Guide to Personal Finance gives you the tools and knowledge you need to build a strong foundation, make informed decisions, and achieve financial freedom. Empower yourself, take action, and create the financial future you deserve. I wish you lifelong financial success and a fulfilling life.

Sincerely,
Christopher Phetlho

ABOUT THE AUTHOR

Christopher Junior

Christopher Junior Kaone Phetlho is an author specializing in non-fiction and educational books, empowering youth in finance. His writing provides practical advice and accessible insights to make learning an enjoyable experience. Christopher is driven by a passion for equipping young individuals with the tools they need for financial success. Inspired by his own journey of overcoming limited resources, he strives to make a positive impact on the lives of others. Through his books, Christopher aspires to shape a brighter future by empowering youth with financial knowledge.

Instagram : @itz_chris_junior

www.ingramcontent.com/pod-product-compliance
Lightning Source LLC
Chambersburg PA
CBHW060852220526
45466CB00003B/1343